Contact Your Spirit Guides

How to Become a Medium, Connect with the Other Side, and Experience Divine Healing, Clarity, and Growth

By: Discover Press

Table of Contents

Introduction

I was born to parents who were medical professionals. Their worldview was scientific and pragmatic. My father, a medical doctor, held a cynical view toward religion and spirituality. Spirits, ESP, psychic powers, and fortune-tellers held no credibility in his eyes. As far as mediums, that was even more far-fetched. It was this mindset that I, through osmosis, absorbed and made my own.

Throughout grade school and my college years, I maintained a purely scientific perspective. If it could not be measured, weighed, or verified, it was just a product of a wild imagination or a weak mind. I had a condescending attitude toward the spiritual domain.

In my mid- to late-twenties, I found myself going through a period where I was unhappy. I felt like something was missing from life. What that was, I did not know. I remember the day that I was doing the dishes in my one-bedroom apartment. The television was on in the living room; it was showing a presentation by Deepak Chopra. He was talking about spirituality.

At first, I just listened to him passively when something changed. I became intrigued by what he was saying. Even more, it resonated with me deeply, though I had no idea what he was talking about. That moment would accumulate with other such moments and would eventually change my life.

I now find myself holding a somewhat rare perspective on life. I can freely embrace both the scientific realm and the spiritual realm. For me, there is no contradiction. My spiritual knowledge continued to deepen, and it led to some amazing spiritual experiences. I have had several out-of-body experiences. I also experienced some moments that I can only describe as belonging to kundalini awakening (This is not my opinion but that of a spiritual teacher that I inquired with).

The deeper my understanding of the spiritual realm became, the more I realized how limited my father's worldview was. I have a whole new perspective toward myself and life. The person I was in the past, before watching that television program, is now a vague memory. For the last 10 years, I have enjoyed a sense of peace and happiness that is unshaken by even the most extreme challenges that I have faced.

The major transformation that I experienced was largely due to my practice of meditation. Meditation provides me with the vehicle to explore higher levels of consciousness. I had studied the nature of consciousness by listening to the lectures of various spiritual teachers. However, through my own meditations, I was able to confirm the validity of their teachings. It was not just confirming the validity of what they spoke of that meditating offered me. It also allowed me to receive my own insights regarding the nature of consciousness and reality.

What I came to realize is the dream-like quality of everyday life. When we dream at night, the dream becomes our reality at that moment. Other than what is contained in the dream, we have no awareness of anything else. In the same way, our experience of reality is like a dream.

Our experience of reality is filled with physical objects that occupy a physical space. We see people carrying on with their daily lives, cars traveling on roads, buildings, and other manmade structures dotting the landscape. There are mountains and forests, oceans and jungles, and plants and animals. All of these things appear in our awareness as aspects of what we refer to as the "real world."

We have experienced other things or have knowledge that seems to belong to a different domain. We do not consider our dreams as being part of reality. Instead, we relegate them to the psychological realm of the mind. In this same manner, death is also treated as part of a different domain. We experience the sadness and the grief of losing someone; however, the afterlife is out of our reach to experience.

Both death and dreams are but fleeting experiences that are confined to our memory or imagination. They are not part of our objective experience of the world. My exploration of higher consciousness levels has confirmed that the nature of reality is far removed from our everyday experience. I remember how we used to watch films in grade school. The teacher turned on the film projector, and the film reels started turning. The projector light then projected the content of the film onto a movie screen. This memory of my childhood is a good metaphor for consciousness. Everything that we experience is a projection of consciousness that presents itself on the screen that we call "reality."

The screen of reality contains all that has ever existed. Each one of us has the inherent potential to explore the screen of reality and tap into the information that is contained in it. For this reason, the metaphysical world that mediums and psychics speak of makes perfect sense to me now.

We live in an information-rich universe that contains data from the beginning of time. Those with extrasensory gifts are simply sampling from this seamless screen of reality, something most of us have yet to do. It is for this purpose that this book was written. It is to provide information on how to develop your psychic abilities and learn to connect with the spirit world.

From my own experience, I can tell you that developing one's psychic abilities brings with it a tremendous amount of personal growth and benefits. More importantly, it allows one to make a greater impact on the world around them by helping others bridge the gap between being caught in a dream and their innate potential to be a more fully actualized being.

Chapter 1: What Are Psychic Powers?

All of us have experienced at one time or another a feeling that something was about to happen, only to find out later that we were right. Or perhaps you thought of someone and then received a phone call from them seconds later. Maybe you experienced an inner voice that told you that you should do something or be somewhere, only to discover later that it was a good thing that you listened to that voice. These are just a few examples where we receive information (a thought or feeling) spontaneously. This information was not associated with any thoughts or feelings that we were experiencing beforehand.

Our normal reaction to these kinds of occurrences is to attribute it to coincidence or common intuition. However, they are actually expressions of psychic power. It is because we dismiss these occurrences as coincidental that we never take time to develop these powers. We often think that psychic powers belong to the realm of mediums, psychics, or mystics. When we experience our own psychic powers, we dismiss them or attribute them to coincidence. At some point, be it in this lifetime or a past one, you have probably chosen to treat these occurrences seriously and are ready to become intentional in cultivating your abilities, and that is why you are reading this book now.

Psychic powers exist within all of us. It is not a question of whether you are psychic or not. Rather, it is about learning where you fall within a range of psychic abilities. Also, you can further develop your psychic abilities, regardless of where you fall in this range.

Many people will tell you that they are intuitive but not psychic. In fact, intuition is actually the essential aspect of all psychic powers. The various forms of psychic powers are just terms for the different ways that information is received through intuition.

We all know what intuition is, and most of us can confidently say that we have experienced it at some point in our lives. Defining intuition is another matter. One of the reasons why defining intuition can be difficult is because we often refer to it by another name. Here are some of the many ways that we refer to intuition:

- I had a hunch…
- I had a gut feeling…
- I listened to my heart.
- I had a feeling that….
- I listened to my inner voice.

Examples of intuitive experiences include:

- You had to make a decision, and you had a feeling as to which would be the best choice.
- You had a feeling that someone you know was in trouble or needed help, though you had no facts or evidence to back up your feelings.
- When the phone rang, you had a knowing as to who the caller was.
- Out of nowhere, you had a thought that you should do something or check up on something.
- You get guidance from within as to what to do in a certain situation.

Intuition can be understood as direct knowing or inner knowing. Direct knowing or inner knowing is a knowing that occurs without us thinking about it. If you are deciding on whether to buy item A or item B, you would normally engage in the process of thinking about it. You may be thinking about the price differences between the two items, the differences in their quality, how your choice will impact your budget and similar lines of thinking.

There are other times when you do not even have to decide. Instantly, you know which item to buy. There is no analysis needed in making your decision. Even if your decision makes no logical sense, you know which item is right for you. Of course, intuition can play a role in an infinite number of other situations.

Intuition is considered a psychic power because it allows us to gain information that our five senses cannot perceive. I remember driving home when I gained information that my wife was upset about something. Other than my intuition, I had no reason to suspect that my wife was unhappy. I had not contacted her, nor were there any issues when I left the house that morning. Further, my intuition came out of the blue. I had not given any thought to my wife's welfare when I was at work that day. Sure enough, when I arrive home, I discovered my wife was indeed unhappy.

Consider your own life:

- How receptive are you to receiving information from your surroundings?
- What type of information or stimuli most deeply resonates with you?
- How does that information or stimuli affect you emotionally?
- How does that information or stimuli affect you physically?
- How does that information or stimuli affect you spiritually?

Imagine that a group of friends plan to meet at a restaurant for dinner. The first friend to arrive at the restaurant approaches the host, leading her to the reserved table. As she sits, she notices that her spot is missing silverware though her water glass is full. She proceeds to take a sip.

Not long after, a second friend arrives at the restaurant. He makes his way to the host's stand. He notices that the host seems oblivious to his presence as her attention is on her cell phone. The second friend politely gets the host's attention. Embarrassed, the host apologizes and leads the second friend to the table. The second friend sits down and greets the first friend.

Sometime later, the third friend arrives. She enters the restaurant and makes her way to the host's stand. As she does so, she starts feeling overwhelmed by the stimuli that fill the establishment. She is aware of the elaborate décor and the hectic motion of the servers. She is aware of the other patrons, especially one of them. This patron is sitting at this table and is talking loudly to the others at his table.

She finds his energy uncomfortable. She perceives him as being arrogant and domineering. She feels sympathy for those who share his table, especially for the woman and children. She wonders what he is like when he is in a private place, as his home. How does he treat his wife and children? When the host announces that she will lead her to her table, the third friend returns to reality. When she arrives at the table, she sits down and shares with her friends her experience.

The last one to arrive, the fourth friend, enters the restaurant. As with the third friend, he, too, is overwhelmed by the stimuli. He picks up the smells, the lights, the sounds, and the movements that are happening there. In seconds, he is aware of the interpersonal dynamics of the patrons who are seated at their tables. He is aware of the coordination between the servers and the kitchen's odors, which bring back childhood memories. He notices that there is damage to the ceiling. The charred rafters inform him that a fire once broke out here. Suddenly he experiences a profound sense of heaviness. Rather than seeing the host, he goes straight to the dining room and heads to the table where his friends are seated.

Though he tries to forget about what he had just experienced, it lingers with him throughout his dinner.

The range of psychic abilities measures the level of sensitivity that we have toward information around us. In the restaurant scenario, the first two friends symbolize the range of information that most of us are sensitive to. We are aware of our surroundings at the gross level, meaning that we know the surface-level information. The first friend is at the low end of the sensitivity range. She picks up the information that there is a host who can lead her to her table. She also picks up the general layout of the restaurant and of the other patrons there. She also was aware of the conversations among the other patrons and the sight of the servers doing their job.

The second friend was a notch higher than the first friend. When he sees the host focused on her cell phone, the second friend is sensitive enough to the information that is coming to him. This information is telling him, "This host is not intentionally ignoring me; she has just misplaced her focus." So the second friend respectfully redirects the host's attention from the cell phone to him.

The third and fourth friends represent the higher end of the range. Their sensitivity allows them to access information that the first two friends were unaware of. In the case of the third friend, the information that they received became overwhelming for them. This same information may have gone unnoticed by the first two friends. If they did notice it, they did not give it a second thought. The reason for this is that they were only superficially tapping into this information.

For the third friend, she was overwhelmed by the sights, smells, and sounds of what she experiences inside the restaurant. She was not only aware of this information, but she was also able to access deeper layers of it, such as the personality type of the boisterous patron.

The fourth friend is a notch above the third friend. His level of sensitivity allowed him to detect everything that the third friend experienced and more. He not only detected the charred ceiling, but he could detect the suffering that resulted from the fire. Further, he had a hard time forgetting about it, even when he was having dinner with his good friends.

The four friends represent both normal sensitivity and extreme sensitivity. Most of us will fall somewhere between these examples. You can evaluate your psychic powers by seeing where you fall in this range of examples.

Later in this book, you will be provided with information on extending your level of sensitivity and increasing your psychic powers. By reflecting on these questions, you can better understand your strengths related to your psychic powers. With this knowledge, you can build on them using the information provided later in this book. In the next section, we will take a closer look at some of the more common psychic powers.

A common question has to do with the difference between intuition and thought. How do you know if the information you are getting is from intuition instead of your thinking? As mentioned earlier, the information from intuition emerges without us having to think about it.

However, there is another way to tell the difference between intuition and thinking. That difference involves the element of emotion. When you think about something relevant to you, it will be accompanied by an emotion. I may meet someone and get a thought that this person cannot be trusted. With that thought, I may feel concerned or fear.

When you tap into your intuition, it will be experienced without any emotional entanglement. It will be just a pure knowing that is received calmly. In fact, having a calm mind will expand your access to your intuition. For this reason, we often have an intuitive moment when we are taking a shower, daydreaming, or simply relaxing.

You and I are multidimensional beings, meaning that we occupy different levels of consciousness at any given moment. At our most essential level, we are pure consciousness. Pure consciousness is consciousness that is free of thought. Pure consciousness is unlimited potential, and it is the source of all manifestations, including ourselves. It also contains all the information of the universe.

In our manifested form, we are individuated expressions of pure consciousness. This means that our physical form is a manifestation of pure consciousness. The unlimited potential of pure consciousness has been restricted so that we can experience the world. This restriction of consciousness is necessary as pure consciousness only experiences oneness. Unlike pure consciousness, which is unlimited in its ability to take in information, we cannot do the same in our manifested forms. The restriction of our awareness is needed to prevent us from becoming overloaded with information.

Intuition is our direct connection to our essential nature. It allows us to tap into the vast storehouse of information that is the pure consciousness. It is for this reason that our intuition lacks an emotional component to it. When we experience intuition, we are experiencing the purity of the higher consciousness realms. The experience of emotions is restricted to our manifested consciousness.

The Four Clairs

There are various ways we receive information via our psychic powers. You can think of these abilities as something like the learning modalities. Some students prefer to learn by listening to a lecture, while others prefer to see real-life examples. Still, others prefer to actually do what is being taught. At the same time, some learn best by participating in a discussion about the topic. In each case, the student can take in the information using the best method for them. The most common forms of psychic abilities are known as the four clairs – clairvoyance, clairaudience, clairsentience, and claircognizance.

When we use our five senses (taste, smell, touch, hearing and sight), we receive information about the physical world. The four clairs are additional ways we receive information about the world around us, past present, and future. The four clairs are clairvoyance, clairsentience, clairaudience, and claircognizance.

Clairvoyance

From French, the word clairvoyance translates to "clear seeing." However, clairvoyance has nothing to do with seeing through the eyes. Rather, it is the intuitive ability to perceive the energy fields around us. Clairvoyance is the information-gathering ability of the 6th chakra, located in the center of the forehead. It is known as the third eye.

The word "chakra" is a Sanskrit word which translates to "wheel." Chakras are the spinning wheels of energy and light. You can imagine a chakra as a whirlpool. A whirlpool is just a configuration of water in motion. In the same way, chakras are the spinning wheels of the spirit.

Have you ever experienced a vision that seemed so real to you that you could not stop thinking about it? Or perhaps you had a dream that really left an impression on you and later became realized. Both of these experiences are examples of clairvoyance. In clairvoyance, your intuition is communicating to you through inner visions or even visual perception.

Most clairvoyants access information using inner visions; however, those who can access information using their normal vision can see energy fields and spirits. We all have the potential to be clairvoyants; however, to transform that potential into ability requires practice.

Those who are clairvoyant tend to be visually oriented. Those who are visually oriented tend to experience intuitive powers as images or visions. Here are some examples of what visually oriented people do:

- When they set a goal, they may visualize its
  achievement in their mind.
- They frequently dream at night.
- They work in the visual arts, including writers and
  directors.
- They have a talent for remembering landmarks or
  other visual cues.
- They will use phrases such as "I see what you mean"
  or "Looks good to me."
- They may speak at a rapid rate.
- When thinking about something, you will notice that
  their eye movements are toward the upper left or
  upper right corner of their eyes.

If you think that you may be clairvoyant, you may want to start
a dream journal to record your dreams each night. You can
then see if they materialize. If you see a pattern of this, you
may be having precognitive dreams.

Clairsentience

While clairvoyants experience the spiritual energy around
them visually, those who are clairsentient experience this
information as feelings. Here are some examples:

- You have a feeling that something is not right.
- You meet someone, and you instantly feel that they
  could be trouble or that this person is someone you
  can't trust.
- You get the feeling someone is watching you.
- You walk into a house and immediately know if it is
  haunted.

- You instantly know the mood of a room when you enter it.
- You hate clutter and need to keep your living area free of it.
- You take your relationships very seriously, and you tend to be very selective as to whom you enter relationships with.

Clairsentients access information from the energy in their surroundings and experience this information as feelings. Children are naturally clairsentient as they are tuned in with their feelings.

Because clairsentients are so in touch with the energy of others, they need to protect themselves from becoming over stimulated. Clairsentients are extra sensitive individuals, and they can easily be overcome by the emotional energy of others. For this reason, these individuals need to learn grounding techniques or psychic shielding.

Tip: Follow up with your intuition. For example, if you feel that a friend is having a bad day, call them up to see if you can verify the accuracy of your feelings.

Clairaudience

While clairsentients experience the spiritual energy around them through the feelings that they receive, those who are clairaudient experience this information through hearing. This auditory guidance can manifest as a voice or music, which is beyond the perception of others. That inner voice that we hear, which is the voice of our intuition, is an example of clairaudience. Those with clairaudience have the potential ability to hear those who have passed on, spirit guides, or angels.

Here are some examples of clairaudience characteristics:

- You love listening to those who are close to you.
- You get great enjoyment listening to the natural world as you attempt to understand it.
- You are a great listener and can give solid and concise advice.
- You can channel spirits through automatic writing.

Tip: Create a sacred space for yourself. When you feel overwhelmed by what you are hearing, go to that space. Announce to yourself that you will only allow those beings with loving intentions to enter your space.

Claircognizance

While clairaudients experience the spiritual energy around them by hearing it, those who are claircognizant experience spiritual energy through knowing it. Claircognizants can find themselves in a new situation, with little information to go by, yet they know what to do. This knowing what to do is acted upon with a great sense of trust and certainty, even though there may be nothing to base it on. Claircognizance is what many experience as a gut feeling.

Examples of claircognizance include:

- You meet some for the first time, yet you feel like you have known them forever. You and the other person feel an instant connection with each other.

- You have a gut feeling telling you what you should do in a situation, even though there is no supporting information to back up that feeling.
- You can make quick decisions.

Psychic powers are the means by which intuition communicates to us. They are the channels by which our intuition shares the boundless information of the universe. Clairvoyance is the channel through which intuition communicates information visually. The same is true with clairaudience, clairsentience, and claircognizance. Each of these is a channel by which the intuition communicates information to us, be it by hearing (clairaudience), feeling (clairsentience), or through knowing (claircognizance).

Many claircognizant people do not realize they are not merely thinking their own thoughts or receiving information from their own intuition, they are in fact practicing mediumship. Their experience of communicating with the spiritual world is easily mistaken for their own thoughts. It takes practice to discern between thoughts that one has and those being communicated by the spirit world. Someone unaware of their psychic powers may believe that their thoughts regarding certain situations are the result of memory.

This is particularly true when it comes to the death of a loved one. A claircognizant may believe that he or she is recalling how the deceased used to think before they passed on. They may not realize that these thoughts could be actual communications from the spirit of the deceased. This brings us to the topics of the next chapter, mediumship and channeling.

Chapter 2: What is a Medium?

Mediums have developed psychic abilities to communicate with those who have passed on to the spirit world. They are the go-between for the afterlife and the world of the living. They tell us what the spirit world has to say while at the same time communicating to the spirit world what we want to know. In this manner, mediums are like a three-way communication channel. The spirit world communicates to the medium while the medium communicates to the information recipient— be it a loved one or other interested parties.

Mediums versus Psychics

The terms medium and psychic are often confused, but there are important differences. The term "psychic powers" is a general term like the word "ice cream," which encompasses all of the flavors available at your local ice cream parlor. Mediumship is one of the major flavors of psychic powers. A major difference between mediumship and other psychic abilities has to do with the receptivity level that each of these abilities requires to gather information from the source energy. While many who use psychic powers are not aware of their special abilities, mediums have taken time to cultivate their talents and use them consciously.

What We Can Learn from Mediums and Their Powers

Everything in the universe is made of energy, and energy has a vibrational quality to it. This can be demonstrated in our daily lives. We can listen to the radio because radio waves, which are a form of energy, are picked up by the radio. If you break your leg and go to the hospital, the x-ray machine used to get a picture of your break uses x-rays. X-rays have a higher frequency than radio waves, so the radio is useless to connect with x-rays. In contrast, an x-ray machine cannot connect with radio waves.

Mediums can raise their energy to a vibrational level that allows them to use their psychic skills to connect with individuals in the afterlife, while psychics use their psychic skills to gather information about a physical object, place, or event. From this information, they receive information about the past, present, or future. However, they cannot raise their vibrational energy high enough to connect with the afterlife as mediums do. For this reason, all mediums are psychic, but not all psychics are mediums.

As mediums are more advanced in their abilities, they can receive detailed information from the individual who has passed. This information demonstrates to the medium's client the validity of the medium's connections with the deceased. Instead of making predictions, mediums provide their client with information from the deceased that will bring about healing.

The Two Kinds of Mediumship

How mediums communicate with spirits varies from medium to medium. There are two major kinds of mediumships; they are mental mediumship and physical mediumship. The type of powers that mediums use to communicate with the spirit world determines which category the medium falls in. Each of these mediumships has its own way in which they communicate with the spirit world. Mental mediumship involves the medium communicating with the spirit world through their mind. In contrast, physical mediums communicate with the spirit world through the manifestation of phenomena. The following is an overview of both.

Mental Mediumship

Mental mediums, commonly known as psychic mediums, receive information from the afterlife through their mental functions. In other words, when the spirit of the deceased communicates with the medium, the information received is experienced as images, visions, verbal messages, and energies. In turn, the medium communicates the message to those who are in attendance. Mental mediums can receive a wide range of factual information from the deceased such as names, location information, and information about their death. The accuracy of the information is determined by the attendees of the session.

Mental mediumship is divided into two groups, control and perception. These two groups indicate how the medium communicates with the spirit world.

Control mediumship is often accomplished by the medium going into a trance. When the medium's mind is taken over by the deceased spirit, it can be an all-consuming experience for the medium, resulting in the medium having no memory of the experience afterward.

In perception mediumship, the medium enters a higher level of consciousness, which allows connection with the deceased's spirit so that she can communicate messages to the living. In control mediumship, the medium allows the deceased's spirit to take over his or her mind. The common forms of perceptual mediumship are known as the four clairs.

They use the four clairs not only to access information about the physical world, but to receive messages from the higher spiritual realms as well. Opening and balancing the chakras can heighten the ability of mediums receive information from the spirit world just as they receive information from the physical environment through the five senses. The different chakras are found in various parts of the body. We will explore the seven chakras later in this book.

Mediums who use clairvoyance connect with the spirit world through visions in their minds or they may see spirits that have taken on physical forms. Clairaudient mediums can hear the voice of a spirit in his or her mind or it may be experienced as a telephone conversation. Clairsentients can feel the energy of a spirit and gain knowledge of a wealth of information about the deceased person. These are all forms of mental mediumship, which occurs within the domain of thought. In other words, communication with the spiritual world is experienced as thoughts.

While our mortal lives may be limited, our information flows continuously from lifetime to lifetime. As a child, your life contained information that informed your decision-making and how you perceived yourself and the world. As you got older, that information followed you as it continued to shape who you are. Upon death, that information continues to travel into the spirit world and eventually becomes incorporated in one's next life.

In this manner, the past information shapes the present moment while the present moment's information shapes the future. When mediums communicate with the spirit world, they are not communicating with the deceased per se. Before my spiritual transformation, I used to believe in the finality of death. When my Aunt Mary passed away, her physical body no longer responded to internal or external stimuli. For me, that was the definition of death.

For myself, as with most people, the death of the body means the death of life. Mediums, and those who are explorers of consciousness, believe otherwise. They believe that there is no such thing as death. Rather, the deceased's life, like Aunt Mary, leaves the body and returns to a higher realm of consciousness, where all of the physical realms originate from. It is like a drop of ocean water that is taken from the ocean. The drop appears to separate from the ocean; however, when the drop returns to the ocean, it becomes one.

Like the ocean, there is a level of consciousness that contains the information of every living being that has ever existed. Mediums tap into this ocean of consciousness and connect with the information that eternally exists there.

Physical Mediumship

While mental mediums communicate with the spirit world through mental activity, physical mediums receive information from the afterlife in physical experiences. A physical medium will pick up sensory information from the deceased, such as odors, feelings, sights, or sounds. For them to receive this information, the physical medium will often go into a trance, which allows them to be more receptive.

As indicated earlier, we all have psychic abilities, though we may not be aware of them. Because of this, we all have the potential to become mental mediums. However, physical mediums are different. Only a few have the potential to become physical mediums. To be a physical medium, one needs to be born with certain aspects, which have yet to be identified.

Whatever these aspects are, they allow for the production of ectoplasm. Ectoplasm is the essential building material from which the physical phenomena are created. Even if one is born with these aspects, it takes a commitment to cultivating the abilities of a physical medium before they can be demonstrated. Another challenge is that being a physical medium requires being very sensitive.

Physical mediumship involves allowing the spirit to temporarily take over one's body. For this reason, the medium must be sensitive to be receptive enough to the spirit's willingness to do so. However, this same level of sensitivity also means that such a person will have a more difficult time dealing with all the craziness of daily life. It is for this reason that physical mediumship is so rarely found today. The following are some of the kinds of physical mediumship that are used by these mediums.

Transfiguration

A rare form of physical mediumship, transfiguration, is a more powerful way of communicating with the dead as the spirit manifests itself using the medium's body. The face of the deceased will actually materialize as an overlay of the medium's face. For this to occur, the medium enters a trance. While in a trance, ectoplasm is released from the medium's body. It is the ectoplasm that takes on the appearance of the deceased's face. Transfiguration requires years of dedicated practice to develop, and it is very draining on the medium. It is for these reasons that transfiguration is rare. It is important to note that many famous instances of ectoplasmic materialization have been found fraudulent. This doesn't mean it never happens or can't happen, but unfortunately it is frequently faked.

Direct Voice

Sometimes the physical medium invites the spirit to communicate through them. When this happens, the spirit expresses itself audibly. In other words, the voice and words of the deceased are emitted from the medium.

When direct voice occurs, the spirit will reconfigure the medium's energy in a way that allows it to manifest a voice of its own. This voice is spoken without the use of the medium's vocal cords. Because of this, the medium and the spirit can carry on a conversation. Direct voice is not the same as channeling. Direct voice mediumship is the easiest form of mediumship to test for its validity. It is so demonstrable when one hears the deceased's voice.

Automatic Writing

In automatic writing, the medium allows the spirit to use them to express themselves through writing. The medium allows the spirit to guide their hand as the message from the afterlife appears as written words. As with other forms of physical mediumship, the medium is often unaware of what is happening until the communication with the spirit has ended. One notable physical medium, Geraldine Cummins, was an author. She used automatic writing to write some of her books.

One of her books, titled *The Scripts of Cleophas*, provided an overview of the rise of Christianity in the first century A.D. During the writing process, she had an assistant who would give her new paper whenever she reached the end of the page. It is interesting to note that Cummins's handwriting changed with each spirit she connected with.

Levitation

Levitation is the phenomenon where a person or object is lifted into the air without any mechanical assistance. Mediums use telekinesis, a form of psychokinetic energy, to make this possible. The most famous physical medium to practice levitation was Daniel Dunglas Home. Born in 1883, Home gave demonstrations of his abilities for over 40 years. In one of his most memorial demonstrations, Home levitated out of a third-story window and then entered another home by its open window. It is said that Home was not always in a trance when levitating. There were periods when he had full awareness of what was happening. When levitating, Home said that he felt an electrical sensation in his feet and that his arms would become extended over his head.

Knocking Sounds

Knocking sounds during a séance is another example of how spirits communicate with physical mediums. The Fox Sisters were most famous for this form of mediumship. The knocks can be used by mediums as a form of a code. The spirit can answer "yes or no" questions posed by the medium by the number of knocks they give.

Apports

During séances or other meetings with a physical medium, there are times when objects appear from nowhere. It is the spirit's way to get the attention of those who are in attendance. The objects are often from other parts of the home. These objects are dematerialized and then reconstructed when they reappear in the space that the attendees occupy. Apports can take the form of any object that was significant to the deceased.

Spirit Lights

Spirit lights are the expressions of spiritual energy that manifests as orbs or flashes of light. Spirit lights arise from our body's chakras, particularly the heart and crown chakra. These lights can be blue, red, or white in color. When these colored orbs move, they may appear as streaks of light. However, we mortals are not the only ones who can emit spirit lights. The spirit world can do the same. Though they are without bodies, those who have crossed over retain the energy of the chakras. Compared to mortal spirit lights, the spirit lights of the deceased are of a larger size as the inhabitants of the spiritual realm have a higher vibrational frequency.

Materialization

Materialization refers to when spirits manifest into physical form. The form that they take on can depict how they appeared before their death or in their current status. The physical representation of the spirit can be extremely detailed. There are cases where even their fingerprints were depicted. When manifested, the spirit may engage with the attendees, even having physical contact with them. The manifested spirit will be linked to the medium by a cord of ectoplasm. It is comparable to an umbilical cord. This cord provides the manifested spirit with energy, which is supplied by the medium. The manifested spirit materializes from the body of the medium. When the spirit is ready to return to the afterworld, it returns via the medium's body.

Ectoplasm

Ectoplasm is an energy-filled substance that originates from within the medium's body. Spirits will mold the ectoplasm to create physical representations of themselves. This is what occurs during transfiguration and materialization. Ectoplasm can also be used by the spirit to move objects. In this sense, ectoplasm can be considered the interface between the spirit world and the physical world.

History of Mediums

Mediums have appeared throughout history, beginning with the Books of Samuel, a volume of the Jewish Tanakh. In the Book of Samuel, Saul seeks the Witch of Endor's services to bring forth the Prophet Samuel's spirit. Saul wants to get advice from Samuel regarding the Philistine war.

The popularity of mediumship took hold in the 19th century with the rise of spiritualism in the United Kingdom and the United States. Notable figures from this time included the three Fox sisters, Paschal Beverly Randolph, and Hippolyte Leon Denizard Rivail.

In New York during the 1800s, Leah, Margaretta, and Catherine Fox enjoyed long successful careers as mediums. They were heavily responsible for the rise of spiritualism in America. Medium Paschal Beverly Randolph was credited for establishing the first Rosicrucian order in the United States. Rosicrucianism is a spiritual movement that originated in 17th century Europe. Among his converts were members of the scientific community, including a chemist, a physicist, an evolutionary biologist, and a Nobel laureate.

Another important medium who lived in the 1800s was the French educator and author Hippolyte Léon Denizard Rivail. Rivail became interested in séances and conducted research on mediums, and eventually became a believer in mediumship. Using the alias Allan Kardec, Rivail coined the term spiritism around 1860. He wrote several books on mediums, including *The Sprits* and *Spiritist Codification*. Later titles included *The Gospel According to Spiritism, Heaven and Hell,* and *The Genesis According to Spiritism.*

The books were largely based on his research which involved observing mediums and answering numerous questions regarding their experiences while communicating with the dead. By the early 1930s, a quarter of million people in the United Kingdom practiced spirituality and there were 2,000 spiritual societies. The popularity of spirituality was also booming in the United States.

Born in the early 1970s, American author Allison DuBois used her psychic abilities to assist law enforcement in solving criminal cases. She did not like to be referred to as a psychic. DuBois felt that the term had negative connotations. She preferred to be called a medium or a profiler. The 2005 to 2011 television series Medium was based on DuBois's life.

Her psychic abilities were tested by Gary Schwartz, director of the VERITAS Research Project at the University of Arizona. The VERITAS Research Project is a journalistic enterprise that investigates corruption in public and private institutions. During one of Schwartz's interviews with DuBois, DuBois informed Schwarz that she had contacted an English woman's deceased husband. When the woman read the interview transcript, she informed Schwartz that 80% of what DuBois said was accurate. Schwartz became a believer in DuBois's abilities.

Other mediums who also became successful television stars were Monica Ten-Kate and Theresa Caputo. Ten-Kate was the star of the television show *Monica the Medium*. It premiered on August 25, 2015, on the television network ABC. The show ran till April 25, 2016. Caputo starred in the television reality show series *Long Island Medium*. The show aired from 2011 to 2019.

Mediumship has always had its critics who believe that communicating with the deceased is impossible and that mediumship is just trickery used to prey upon the unsuspecting. Scientific researchers have used controlled studies to test the medium's abilities; however, they are often inconclusive in their findings.

While many research studies have used detailed protocols to set up the experiments, there is a question of whether mediums can perform under the methodology's rigor. It could be that authentic mediums exist; however, they cannot use their abilities under such conditions. Further, even the researchers admit that there are so many variables involved when studying mediums that they have difficulty controlling them all.

In Tucson, Arizona, there is a research center that takes mediums seriously. Researchers at Windbridge Research Center study ways to ease the suffering caused by the death of a loved one. They use medical and mental health clinicians, scientists, and mediums to conduct rigorous research. They study ways to reduce anxiety related to death, the nature of end-of-life experiences, treatment for grief, and to understand the practices used by mediums and other practitioners.

Channeling

While mediumship involves acting as the intermediary between the departed and their loved ones, channeling involves connecting with the afterworld for more philosophical purposes. It may involve connecting with the spirit of someone we did not know, such as a historical figure. Channeling is a craft that needs to be approached with greater caution as we would not have any historical record to validate the information that the mediumship is offering.

Channeling is a form of communication that mediums use to gather information from the spirit realm; however, it can also be used with animals. When mediums practice channeling, they become an interpreter between the spirit and those in attendance. The spirit communicates by thoughts and feelings as verbal communication is not needed at higher levels of consciousness. When this information is received by the medium, he or she experiences this information in the form of words.

This method of exchanging information brings about an important point. Channeling occurs more often than we may think. When we experience thoughts, we believe that they originated from us. Some of our thoughts may be the result of us channeling, but we are unaware of it. Channeling explains how people who do not know each other may develop the same ideas for fashion, music, art, and inventions.

For channeling to occur there must be willingness by both the spirit and those attending the channeling session to give or receive information. It is incorrect to believe that the spirit needs to occupy the medium's body for channeling to occur. Often the spirit can be light-years away and still communicate with the medium.

When it comes to animals, channeling is easier to perform. The reason for this is that animals, especially pets, want to communicate with humans. Instead of using thought, animals communicate information through feelings. If you want to channel your pet, allow yourself to feel what your pet tries to communicate to you. As you become open enough to receive the animal's feelings, you will start receiving the information in the form of words.

To communicate with the animal, express yourself through your feelings. In the beginning, you may want to visualize the animal or have a picture of it. This will help you connect with the animal. As you become more proficient, you will not need to visualize the animal or use a photograph. More than anything, it takes practice to be able to perform channeling.

Another form of psychic power is the ability to communicate with spirit guides. As this topic covers so many areas, the next chapter is dedicated to it.

Chapter 3: Spirit Guides

The concept of spirit guides has been around since ancient civilizations. Even before the expansion of Christianity and Islam, spirit guides were deeply entrenched in traditional African culture. To this day, many Africans believe that the spirits of their ancestors live on eternally, providing them with guidance and protection. Spirit guides are seen as the go-betweens of the living and God.

In Western culture, spirit guides are not necessarily the descendants of humans as there are numerous other spiritual types. Some spirit guides exist as energy or light beings and inhabit the cosmic domain, having never inhabited our earthly plane. From a western perspective, spirit guides are energetic beings who have fulfilled their life purpose and have taken on the role of a protector or guide to the living. The following are descriptions of the more common spirit guides.

Guardian Angels and Life Guides

Each one of us has a guardian angel that has opted to serve us. Guardian angels assist us by helping us accomplish our life's purpose. These spirit guides have a high vibrational frequency; hence, their dominant qualities are that of unconditional love. Their high vibrational frequency enables them to provide us with wisdom and knowledge when needed.

Since their vibrational level is much higher than ours, our vibrational level rises in response to theirs. This increase in our vibrational level allows their knowledge and wisdom to be received by us. Unlike other kinds of spirit guides, guardian angels are always with us.

Similar to guardian angels, life guides play more of an organizational role. They coordinate all the other spirit guides so that the right ones are always available to ensure that your life does not get too crazy. An important thing to remember with life guides, as with all guides, is that you need to be open to receive their messages. As powerful as they may be, they cannot supersede your free will. If we are not receptive to their guidance, we can experience our lives becoming overwhelming.

Divine Timing Guides

We may believe that we are free-willed beings who can choose freely and shape our destiny. This perception is warranted, given the level of our conscious awareness. However, at higher levels of consciousness, everything that we hold as being true falls apart at these higher realms. Such a realm of consciousness is where the divine timing guides reside.

These spirit guides are the ones that possess the master plan of our lives. Unbeknownst to us, everything that we experience was predestined. Divine timing guides are the ones that are in charge of seeing that everything that happens in your life happens at the right time. Divine timing guides also are the ones behind our experience of synchronicity. It is important to note that you and I are not separate entities from the divine timing guides or any other guide, for that matter.

At our most essential level, we are pure consciousness. How we experience ourselves is the physical manifestation of pure consciousness. What this means is that we are multidimensional beings who are simultaneously a conscious being and consciousness itself. It is for this reason that the idea of having free will while at the same time having our lives preplanned are not incompatible realities. We will explore the different levels of consciousness in a later chapter.

Protector Guides

Also known as warrior guides, protector guides can be compared to bodyguards. However, instead of dealing with individuals who harbor ill intent, protector guides protect us from psychic energy that may be harmful to us. Besides protecting us from spiritual attacks, protector guides also protect our mental and physical welfare.

As with guardian angels, protector guides have a very high frequency. It allows them to protect us from guidance or advice that may cause us to deviate from the direction of achieving our higher purpose. When we experience the thought or feeling that something is amiss, it is a message from our protector guide.

Creative Guides

If you ask an artist, a musician, or a writer where they get their creative ideas come from, many of them will tell you that it just came to them. The artist will tell you that he or she just had a knowing of how to approach their artwork. The musician would tell you that their music came through them, just as the writer would say that the words flowed through them.

In all of these cases, the person's artistic endeavors came largely from the guidance of their creative guides. These artistic individuals were open to receiving the creative energy provided by these guides. Creative guides do not just serve artists. They can serve each one of us if we are willing to be open to their guidance. Creative guides are available to us for problem-solving or decision-making. Creative guides can get us to view life through a new perspective that provides us opportunities to come up with answers that are outside of the realm of ordinary thinking.

Gatekeeper Guides

Like the protector guides, gatekeeper guides also protect us by guarding us against influences that may harm us physically or psychically. Additional gatekeeper guides are also the stewards of the Akashic records. The Akashic records are the storehouse for all information regarding the past, present, and future.

Teacher Guides

The role of teacher guides is to teach us lessons that will keep us from straying from our path. Each of us follows a path that will lead to our understanding of our life's purpose. The experiences that we have each day are all created by the spirit world to guide us to a deeper understanding of our essential truth and that of reality itself.

When we awaken to these truths, we will be liberated from the sufferings that come with the belief that we are a limited and separate self. It is this journey of self-discovery that the teacher guides provide us with the lessons that will keep us on the path that is correct for us. The lessons that teacher guides provide us can be found in our dreams, meditations, or subtle signs that we encounter in everyday life.

At the most fundamental level, the teacher guides are our experiences, both good and bad. It is important to remember that "good" and "bad" are the exclusive products of the mind. There is nothing in life that is inherently good or bad. It is just us who form judgments and impose them on our experiences. In this manner, life is a continuous feedback loop that is informing us as to whether we are moving forward on our path or if we lost our way.

Happiness Guides

What is that every person ultimately wants? The answer is joy or happiness. Our challenge is that we so often pursue those things that we believe will bring us happiness instead of noticing the happiness within us. Happiness guides are creative in their way to get us to redirect our focus from our perceived concerns to experience the joy that naturally exists within us all.

You cannot know anything in life unless you already have knowledge of its existence. Someone may be pursuing money or a relationship because they believe obtaining these things will make them happy. However, the happiness experienced when our desires are fulfilled does not come from the object of our desire.

The happiness we feel comes from within us. The object of our desire was just a stimulus to cause us to reveal our happiness. We know happiness because happiness is who we are at the most fundamental level. When we become consumed by our concerns or worries, the happiness guides do their magic. They get us to change our perspective and notice all the things we can be happy about in our world. Happiness guides get us to notice those things that awaken the joy within us.

Healing Guides
It is the nature of the spirit or consciousness to be stress and disease-free. Stress and disease are phenomena that only occur on this earthly plane and are the product of our minds. The human body is naturally exposed to diseases but can tolerate them as long as it remains in equilibrium. Stress, which the mind creates, disrupts the body's equilibrium and allows the disease to gain the advantage.

Healing guides lead us to healing by getting us in touch with the body's natural healing energies. By getting us to refocus on health, as opposed to the experience of stress, healing guides lead us back to the body's natural wellbeing. In the same manner, healing guides get us to shift our focus on emotional and mental healing instead of placing our attention on our disempowering thoughts. Similarly, healing guides can lead us back to spiritual wellness.

Healing guides can originate from the Earth, or they may belong to an entity that has moved beyond our worldly plane. Spiritual healers, ancient monks, modern medical practitioners, and old-world shamans are examples of healing guides that inhabit or once inhabited Earth. Those healing guides who no longer inhabit the Earth would include ascended masters or archangels. Jesus and Archangel Raphael are examples of this category of healing guides.

Ascended Masters are individuals who have become enlightened and are no longer bound by space and time. They have escaped the cycle of birth, life, and death. It is this achievement that separates them from those who have passed on but are still trapped in the cycle of birth, life, and death. Most likely, you have encountered your healing guides in the past. It may not have been obvious to you because healing guides are resistant to revealing their true nature as they are extremely humble.

Spirit Animal Guides

Spirit animal guides are ascended beings who offer us guidance, protection, and assistance. They are deeply grounded in nature, and their mission is to guide us in keeping our energy grounded as well. From the Native American perspective, spirit animals are the manifestation of a spiritual guide. The spirit animal guide that enters our lives possesses qualities that mirror our own. However, they may be latent within us. In this way, our spirit animal is reminding us of what we possess already. If we took advantage of these qualities, we would be able to experience life with greater ease, enjoyment, and success.

Spirit animal guides are an important part of the Native American belief system. They come to us during times of great change. They guide us through times of uncertainty by teaching us the wisdom of their species. For example, if the spirit animal was a wolf, it would teach us the wisdom of the wolf.

Spirit animals do not teach by the use of words. Instead, it is up to us to discern the wisdom of the animal in how it survives. Spirit animal guides can appear in our dreams or meditations. Each person has their own spirit animal. Additionally, there are four kinds of animal guides. These include shadow spirit guides, messenger guides, life guides, and journey guides.

Shadow Spirit Guides

Shadow spirit guides are animals that come to those of us who have unresolved fears or insecurities in our lives. These shadow animals will keep appearing in our lives until we have learned to overcome our fears through positive change. If one ignores their spirit animal, his or her negative energy will continue to grow.

Messenger Guides

Messenger guides enter our lives in order to warn us of approaching dangers to our wellbeing. Besides warning us, they also offer guidance on how to avoid the situation. They will continue to appear until we have understood what they are trying to communicate to us.

Life Guides

Unlike the other three animal guides, life guides remain with you throughout your life. However, during the course of your life, you may have more than one life guide. This type of animal guide is a reflection of your current standing in life. They serve to remind you of your strengths and potentials. Frequently, life guides take the form of an animal that we have a fondness for.

Journey Guides

When arriving at the fork in the road of one's life, journey guides appear. They will remain with you until you have made the decision of which road to take and have successfully completed your journey.

As any animal can be a spirit guide, this book cannot cover every spirit animal guide. Instead, here is a shortlist of spirit animal guides as examples:

Butterfly
The butterfly represents transformation and growth. It is also characterized by being very adaptable to change and the ability to approach uncertainty with grace.

Cat
The cat signifies independence, great patience, adventure, and curiosity.

Dove
The dove symbolizes peace, hope, optimism, and beginning a new.

Elephant

The elephant represents wisdom and gentleness. It also signifies spiritual understanding.

Horse

The horse epitomizes passion, drive, productivity, and being goal-oriented.

Lion

The lion is a natural leader with a sense of deep-seated authority, heart, and courage.

Owl

The owl is astute in its ability to see things that are overlooked by others. In other words, it is able to discern the deeper meaning of things along with those less than obvious life treasures.

Wolf

The wolf is the hallmark of primal instinct, intelligence, and freedom.

How to Identify your Spirit Animal Guide

Now that you have an idea about what spirit animal guides are all about, here are some tips on how to identify which animal is your spirit guide:

Dream Journaling

Whenever an animal appears in your dreams, write it down in your journal. Make this the first thing that you do after waking up. If you put off documenting your dreams, you may forget their contents.

After you have recorded your dreams for a period of time, check to see if there is any consistency in your dreams. Does the same animal repeatedly appear in your dreams? If so, that is a strong indication that it is your spirit animal guide.

Do you have an animal that you have a special affinity for? Is there an animal species that you feel a strong connection with? Perhaps you have had a special pet or a chance encounter with an animal that has had a lasting impression on you. If so, this also points to it as being your spirit animal guide.

Animal Journaling

Find some time when you can be alone for about five minutes without interruption. In your journal, write about an animal that you feel connected to. Ask yourself the following question, "Presuming that this animal is my spirit guide animal, what is it here to teach me about my personal power and potential? What is it here to teach me about my inner strength?"

Take a few minutes to write down whatever comes to you. Trust whatever appears in your mind, even if it does not make sense to you at the moment. After each exercise, revisit it the following day by reading what you wrote. See if any of the teaching points that you wrote down seem relevant to you. Repeat this exercise over a period of a few weeks or even a month. You do not have to use the same animal each time if another animal species attracts your attention. By doing this exercise, you will be able to check for patterns in the teaching points that you have recorded.

Learning the Lessons from your Spirit Animal Guide

Now that you have identified your spirit animal, your next step is to learn how to receive their lessons. Your spirit animal is a reflection of you. Your spirit animal's characteristics that allow it to thrive are the same characteristics that we should be expressing in our own lives at this moment in time. This is an important distinction as your spirit animal can change when the times call for it. The spirit animal that you need to learn from will always appear in your life when the situation is right.

To reinforce the message that your spirit animal is sending you, you can get a representation of your spirit animal (a photograph, painting, or figurine) and place it where you will see it every day. Doing this will remind you of your spirit animal's qualities. The practice of using a representation of your spirit animal is what some Native American tribes do when they create animal totems.

The appearance of your spirit animal, be it in real life or as a representation, is intended to remind you of its powerful characteristics that will benefit you if you adopt them in your own life.

Having discussed how you can learn the lessons from your animal spirit guides, we will next discuss how to communicate with your spirit guides in general.

Ways that You Can Receive Your Spirit Guide's Messages

How spirit guides communicate with us can be subtle, so it is important to be attentive to your environment so that you can pick up on their signs. In fact, we may often experience things that we dismiss as coincidental when they are a message from our spirit guides. What is commonly known as synchronicity is actually our spirit guides sending a message to us. For example, say that you are having problems in your relationship. You decide to get into your car and go for a drive so that you can unwind.

As you drive, you pass a billboard that is advertising an upcoming seminar by a relationship expert. This could be a message from your spirit guides. Other ways spirit guides can communicate to us is through numbers or music. Perhaps you have an interview with an employer, and you notice that your lucky number is included in the company's address. Maybe you had a bad day at work. At the end of the workday, when you're driving home, an inspiring song comes on the radio.

Another way that spirit guides communicate with us is to place certain people or opportunities on our path that will benefit us. Or we can receive messages from our spirit guides through meditations or dreams.

The following section has tips for recognizing the messages from your spirit guides.

Become Mindful
It is difficult to pick up on our spirit guides' messages if you are caught up in your thinking mind. It is important to learn to

be present in your daily life so that you can experience your surroundings instead of your mind's activities.

In order to learn to be more mindful, take up meditation (meditation will be covered later in this book). In the meantime, take time each day to be quiet. Place your attention on your breathing or your surroundings. If you take time to spend in nature, even if it's just your backyard or a park, you will find becoming mindful is a lot easier than being indoors.

Become Intentional

As you go through your day, be intentional in your search for signs from your spirit guides. The more intentional you are when looking out for signs from your spirit guide, the more you will spot them. Additionally, the more you can detect your spirit guides' messages, the more they will send them out to you.

Take time daily to look for signs from your spirit guides. Your spirit guides can send you messages at any time. Even the simple act of taking a shower can be an opening for your spirit guides to communicate with you.

Remember, we are more likely to receive our spirit guides' guidance when our minds are relaxed. However, a prime time for receiving signs from your spirit guides is when you are facing challenges, going through major changes, or when you have to make important decisions. Pay particular attention during these times to guidance from the spiritual realm.

Keep a Spirit Journal

Each day, write in your journal what you experienced during your day as it relates to any potential signs that you received. Also, indicate any challenges that you may be going through or any uncertainties that you are facing.

See if you can draw a connection between your life's situation and the signs you received. Also, if you have unresolved questions about any aspect of your life, write out your questions and pose them to your spirit guides. Ask them for guidance in these matters. As you get answers from your spirit guides, document them in your journal as well.

Review each day what you wrote the day before. See if you can match up the signs you received with the questions that you notated in the past. By documenting and reviewing each day, you will pick up patterns between the messages you receive and your life's situations.

Practice Surrender

The essence of who we are is pure consciousness. All that we experience, including our experience of ourselves, are the projections of pure consciousness in manifested form. For these reasons, you and I are multidimensional beings. Our essential nature is the spiritual realm, while our manifested being exists in the physical realm.

When we are facing challenges, we can become entangled in our thoughts. We worry about what might happen in the future or spend time analyzing the problem or strategizing ways to deal with the problem. All of this thinking cuts us off from the spiritual realm. We are unable to receive the messages from our spiritual guides. Practicing surrender will allow you to regain your connection to the universe's spiritual energies and receive their guidance.

The next time you find yourself facing a challenge, take the time to interrupt your busy mind and surrender to your situation. Taking time just to surrender will slow down your mental activity and allow the access to your spirit guide's messages.

Educate Yourself About Spirit Guides

Learn more about spirit guides by reading up on them or take a workshop. The more you become familiar with them, the more effective you will be in receiving their guidance.

Cultivate your Intuition

It was stated earlier that everyone has psychic powers. Psychic powers are the ability to listen to your intuition. Your intuition is your connection with the realm of pure consciousness. The four Clairs (clairvoyance, clairaudience, claircognizance, and clairsentience) are four different ways to receive information from our intuition.

Learn to cultivate your intuitive abilities by practicing them in real-life situations. You can do this by making more decisions, especially those decisions that are inconsequential to you. For example, let's say you and a friend are talking about going out for lunch. Make a decision as to where you want to go and see how your lunch experience turns out.

By making small decisions like these and evaluating those decisions' outcomes, you can become more adept at differentiating your intuitive knowing and cognitive thinking. As you gain confidence in your ability to trust your intuition, you can apply them to more meaningful decision-making.

Develop a Spiritual Practice
Develop a spiritual practice such as yoga, meditation, prayer, or join a spiritual group. The more you become in tune with the spiritual aspect of yourself, the more easily you will receive spiritual guidance. Learning meditation is a great practice because it provides unlimited opportunities to improve your understanding of your mind and higher consciousness levels.

Ask, and You Will Receive
It was previously noted that spiritual journaling can be used to write down your questions or concerns and see if you get a message from your spiritual guide. This same thing can be done by asking the spiritual realm for help. Whether it is through prayer, meditation, or when you can take a moment to be still, ask your spiritual guides for guidance. After asking, do not give any thought about the matter and resume your normal activities. When you do this, you are practicing detachment.

Detachment means that you are taking a break from thinking about the issues you are facing. You are not waiting or anticipating a response from your spirit guides. By doing this, you are providing access for yourself to receive guidance from your spiritual guides.

As stated before, we are multidimensional beings. When we practice stillness through prayer, meditation, or other means, we increase our vibrational frequency. The increase in our vibrational frequency places us in greater alignment with higher consciousness levels. When this occurs, accessing information from the higher conscious realm becomes easier.

Chapter 4: The Spiritual Realm

We live in an energetic universe. Everything that exists in the universe is made up of energy. Even those objects that seem solid are composed of energy. In classical physics, also known as Newtonian physics, it is believed that everything is made of matter. Matter is a substance that has mass and volume. Mass is defined as the amount of matter in an object.

Volume is the amount of space that the object occupies. Atoms were considered to be the smallest unit of matter. Based on this perspective, you and I are made of matter in that we have mass, which can be measured by our weight and volume, in that we take up space. Further, we could say that the smallest unit that we are composed of is the atom.

The advent of quantum physics dismantled the principles of classical physics. From the perspective of quantum physics, the atom is not solid; rather, it is a fluctuation of energy.

Energy is not solid, nor does it have mass or volume. Because of this, everything we experience is an expression of energy.

The illusion of physicality comes from our limited sensory ability to discern an energetic universe's substratum. It is like when we look into a mirror. The reflection that we see in the mirror appears to be a solid physical body made of flesh and bone. However, the body is made of trillions of microscopic cells. In turn, each cell is made of numerous cell components.

These components are made of smaller components. In turn, these smaller components are made up of even smaller components, and so on. Diving down deeper, we would eventually reach the atomic level. Go down even further, and you guessed it…. all that we would find is energy.

The energy that I speak of is not to be confused with the energy we use in our daily lives to power our homes or run our vehicles. Instead, the energy that I speak of has intelligence, and it contains information. It is this intelligence and information that creates the unlimited expressions of life that we experience. It is for this reason that we can refer to this energy as conscious energy or Prana. Whether it is a cell from the human body, an embryo, or a rock, this energy provides the blueprint for the physical world to take form.

However this energy manifests, its manifestation is not separate from this energy. You are not only a manifestation of this energy; you are inseparable from it. It is like a drop from the ocean and the ocean itself. The drop shows no resemblance to the mighty ocean; however, the drop and the ocean are identical in their chemical composition. In the same way, you are inseparable from the universe. It is only in our minds that we make distinctions between these two.

Whether it is a constellation in the evening sky, the mighty Himalayan Mountains, or bacteria, the essence of who we are is one with all of these things. Everything that we can experience is found within conscious energy, and everything that we experience is conscious energy.

The manifestation process is the natural outcome of a vibrational universe. All that is created has a vibrational quality to it. Imagine the strings of a guitar, violin, or any other stringed instrument. Each string vibrates at a specific frequency, which is why each string creates a unique sound of its own. The tighter the string is, the higher the frequency of the sound that it creates. Conversely, the looser the string is, the lower the frequency of its sound. Like the guitar string, everything in this universe has its own frequency due to its energetic vibration.

While consciousness is the essence of existence, every expression of consciousness has its own vibrational frequency. To better understand this, we can use the hydrologic cycle as a metaphor. Water can take on the form of a gas, a liquid, or a solid. What determines the form that the water takes on is the behavior of its molecules.

In the gaseous state, the water molecules are further apart than in any other state. The reason why water is invisible as gas is because of the great distances between its molecules. They are also very active because they vibrate at a high frequency.

When water becomes a liquid, the molecules are closer together, but still have a great distance. It is for this reason, water, as a liquid, can flow and take on the shape of the container that it is in. As a liquid, the molecules are active and vibrate at a high frequency. However, their activity and vibrational frequency are lower than that of a gas.

When water becomes solid, the molecules are close together. It is the close proximity of the molecules that gives ice its solid form. Because of their close proximity, the molecules are far less active than liquid water and have a low vibrational rate. Just as with water, the different manifestations of consciousness also have a vibrational quality to them.

As long as we are caught up in the belief that we are just a physical body separate from the rest of the universe, our vibratory rate will be low, just like ice. From this state, it will be difficult to experience our psychic abilities. When we raise our awareness and realize that we are spiritual beings, we will be like water vapor. Our vibratory levels will significantly increase. We will be able to connect with our psychic powers.

The frequency of our lives determines how open we are to receiving communications from the spiritual realm. To cultivate our psychic abilities, we must learn to raise our vibratory level. Later in this book, we will explore ways to raise our vibrational frequency. In the next section, we will examine how the vibratory quality of energy creates the different planes of consciousness.

The Seven Planes of Existence

The number seven is significant in understanding the vibratory nature of the universe. Rainbows have seven colors. There are seven levels of energy that create the atom, and there are seven tones on the musical scale. In all of these examples, the number seven refers to the number of different frequency levels found in these things. Each color of the rainbow has its own frequency, as do each of the atom layers and tones.

Each of these planes has its own level of vibrational frequency, creating its own dimension within the conscious energy field. The higher the plane, the higher its vibrational frequency will be. The lower the plane, the lower its vibrational frequency. At the lower frequency range, manifestations occur, including the manifestation of thoughts and the physical body. This means that our physical world is at the lowest plane while the spiritual realm is found in the higher planes. The Seven Planes are the Physical Plane, the Astral Plane, the Causal Plane, the Akashi Plane, the Mental Plane, the Messianic Plane, and the Heavenly Plane.

The Physical Plane

The Physical Plane is the dimension of the physical world. It is also the plane where the experience of space and time exists. This is also the plane where there is a deep identification with the mind and body. The essence of who we are is conscious energy; however, the vibrational frequency of our manifested selves is at the low end of the scale.

We, as consciousness, experience these low-frequency energies as the physical body. Further, the quality of our consciousness also is affected. We are unbounded pure consciousness at our most fundamental level. This means that there are no limitations to our awareness. However, at the level of the Physical Plane, our conscious awareness is limited. The reason for this is that we appear in this dimension to have experiences. It is our experiences that inform the higher planes of consciousness as to the nature of itself. It is for this reason that we find ourselves in this first domain, the Physical Plane.

Pure consciousness cannot have experiences as it knows only oneness. To have an experience requires a sense of separation between the observer and the observed. The experience of having a body creates a sense of separation between us and what we are experiencing.

Because our consciousness is limited, we identify with our mind and physical body. This sense of identification leads us to believe that we are separate entities in a physical world with other entities. The self-identification with the mind and body, along with our sense of separateness, informs the highest plane, the Heavenly Plane, of its own nature. In other words, the conscious universe has a feedback loop that allows it to receive information about itself. The source of that information comes from the Physical Plane.

The Astral Plane

The Astral Plane is the second level of consciousness. It is the plane where the soul travels to when one has died. This is the level of consciousness where the soul exists between the times it leaves the Physical Plane and its next lifetime. For those who experienced physical death, the Astral Plane is the first stop along the journey to the highest realms of consciousness. This is also the dimension experienced by those who have had out-of-body experiences (OBE).

No longer burdened by the physical body, the spirit no longer experiences a sense of separation. To experience the Astral Plane, we need to raise our vibrational frequency. This is what mediums do when they practice mediumship. They raise their vibrations so that they can make contact with higher planes, including the Astral Plane.

This dimension is not inhabited exclusively by the deceased's soul, for there are other spiritual beings that reside there as well. Other residents of the Astral Plane include non-human entities. These include lower-level spirit guides and elementals. In fact, any entity that is found on the Physical Plane can be found in the Astral Plane, minus its physical form.

The Astral Plane is divided into its own separate layers, with one layer having a higher frequency than the other. These two layers are the equivalent of Heaven and Hell; they are inhabited by residents who vary in their temperaments and in their intentions. Those inhabitants with negative temperaments or intentions are found in the lower frequency layer. In contrast, those with good temperaments and intentions occupy the higher frequency layer. The following entities are found in the Astral Plane:

> **Elementals:** The basic elementals are fire, earth, and water. As indicated before, everything that can be found on Earth (the Physical Plane) can be found in the Astral Plane. However, it will appear in a non-physical form. This is true of the basic elements.

Spirit Guides: Because of their benevolent nature, spirit guides are found in the upper layer of the Astral Plane.

Demons: Demons have low vibrational frequencies; hence, they appear at the lower level.

Fiends: These inhabitants possess negative energy. Because of their tendencies to create chaos, mediums are careful not to engage these entities.

Parasites: These entities feed on the energy of other entities, in particular human spirits that have a lower life state. Though the residents of the Astral Plane appear as energy, they retain the information from their life on the Physical Plane. The spirits of humans who were unable to emotionally heal themselves from their sufferings or tragedies will retain this information. Such spirits are vulnerable to parasites.

Human Spirits: The spirits of humans may remain in the Astral Plane to deepen their knowledge of this conscious realm, or they will stay as they wait for family members to join them. Those who decide to stay are the spirits most likely to be contacted by mediums. Those who decide not to say may go to higher planes of consciousness or reappear on the Physical Plane.

The return to the Physical Plane occurs in those spirits who experience rebirth. What determines whether they are reborn is their karma. If such spirits would benefit from having their karma changed, they will be reborn to the Physical Plane. Those who stay in the Astral Plane can create major changes on Earth by altering the Earth's vibrational frequency.

Causal Plane

The Causal Plane is the third-highest plane, and it contains the Akashic Records. While inhabiting the Physical and Astral Planes, we are interacting with our environment. In the Physical Plane, we interact with the world of form. In the Astral Plane, we, as the spirit, interact with the nonphysical realm. Either way, these interactions create information.

The information obtained from our interactions becomes part of universal energy. The third law of thermodynamics states that energy cannot be created or destroyed. It is for this reason that the Akashic records can hold information about our past lives. These past lives include those that occurred both in the Astral Plane and the Physical Plane.

In the Astral Plane, past lives mark the evolution of consciousness. In other words, learning is occurring. The energy of the universe has intelligence as it contains information. As learning occurs, consciousness expands. The state of consciousness before a given expansion is considered a past life. The Akashic Records house information on our past lives in the Astral and Physical Planes. Highly skilled mediums can tap into the Causal Plane.

Akashic Plane

The Akashic Plane is unusual in that it is neutral. It has neither a positive nor negative vibratory frequency. It is also interconnected with the other six planes. While the Causal Plane contains information of the Physical and the Astral Planes, the Akashic Plane contains the information of the entire universe. Everything that occurs in the universe is stored in the Akashic Plane. This information is captured at the moment that it occurs. When information reaches the Akashic Plane, it is assimilated and distilled by consciousness and then retained there.

The Akashic Plane is like a library with an infinite amount of information regarding every aspect of the universe. Obtaining information from this library requires a high vibrational frequency. Mediums who have honed their skills to a high level can access that information similar to those who carry out astral projections. We all can access this library; however, cultivating that ability requires a determined effort. As each person has their own vibrational frequency, the time that it takes to achieve this ability will vary from person to person. It may occur in this lifetime for some, while for others, it may take more than one lifetime.

Mental Plane
The fifth plane of existence, the Mental Plane, is very similar to the Causal Plane as both are informational energy sources. The difference is that the Mental Plane contains a higher level of energy. The energy of the Causal Plane relates to past and future events, for this is how the mind of the human species is oriented. Most of our thoughts involve thinking about the past or the future.

In the Mental Plane, the available information is that of the present moment. Both past and future are illusionary in that they do not reflect true reality. Instead, the past and future are the creations of the human mind. At higher levels of consciousness, time ceases to exist. Given that the information contained in the Mental Phase is based on the present moment, it is based on true reality.

For this reason, the energy in this dimension is referred to as pure thought. It is for this reason that the Mental Phase has a higher vibrational frequency. The Mental Plane is considered to be where God resides.

Messianic Plane

The Messianic Plane is the second-highest plane of consciousness and is characterized by unconditional love. There is a love for all beings. It is in this dimension that there is recognition of the unity consciousness as there is only oneness. This plane offers direct contact with the Divine and an understanding of the infinite. The incarnations from the Messianic Plane include Jesus.

Heavenly Plane

The highest plane of consciousness is the Heavenly Plane. This plane is characterized by pure energy. The Buddha was the incarnation of the infinite soul that came from this plane. When the soul reaches this dimension, it has reached the end of its journey. The soul can either merge with the infinite or return to a lower plane, including that of the Earth, and be reborn as a new life. When this happens, the soul will take on a new vibrational frequency and take on a new physical form or remain formless.

You and the Spirit World are One

The Seven Planes of Consciousness are a model of consciousness. Everything that exists is found within consciousness, is made of consciousness, and contains consciousness. Consciousness is a form of energy that contains intelligence and information. To say consciousness has intelligence is to say that it is dynamic. Consciousness is continually seeking to expand and evolve. To do so, it needs to create contrast within itself. Contrast is what creates dynamic activity. How could you know what light is if you had no knowledge of the dark? How could you know peace if you never knew war? The conscious universe learns about itself by creating contrast within itself.

To review, the Heavenly Plane is of oneness and unconditional love. Conversely, the Physical Plain is characterized by separateness and fear. Separateness is created by the consciousness manifesting a physical body and then identifying with that body. This sense of identification creates the perception that anything outside of the body must be something other than oneself.

The sense of being a separate self that exists in a world creates contrast. Having forgotten its essential nature, the illusionary self focuses its attention outward. By doing so, it forms attachments to the world of form. The ego-based mind leads to the entity believing that it needs something that exits outside itself to experience fulfillment. It is for this reason that we seek relationships, status, power, or money.

We have the belief that if we can obtain these things that we will feel whole. In truth, what we are missing is our connection to our essential self, the highest level of consciousness, the Heavenly Plane.

The separate self, also known as the illusionary self, will continue its pursuit to find fulfillment by seeking it out in the physical realm. To reach the higher planes of consciousness, the separate self needs to either surrender the pursuit of fulfillment or experience the body's death. At some point, the separate self will realize that the obtainment of anything within the Physical Plane will not bring lasting fulfillment. When this point is reached, the entity will eventually look inward and discover a deeper realm, the spiritual realm. The other option is that the entity will die. The consciousness will be liberated from its identification with the physical body.

Whether it is from looking inward or from being liberated from death, the spirit, which is also an aspect of consciousness, will experience an increase in its vibrational frequency. The increase in vibrational frequency is due to the diminished sense of identification with the physical body. This results in the consciousness traveling to the Astral Plane. The Astral Plane is a mirror of the Physical Plane, though it does not contain its physicality.

Just as in the Physical Plane, spiritual entities (meaning those that lack physical form) interact with each other, just as they did in the Physical Plane. These interactions generate new information, which is collected by the Akashic Records of the Causal Plane. As energy cannot be created or destroyed, the information found in the Akashic records provides information on what is known to us as "past lives." In truth, there is no such thing as past lives.

The concept of past lives exists only in the Physical Plane as it is only there that the concept of time exists. Since energy is eternal, and there is no concept of time in the higher planes, the Astral Plane contains information on everything that has ever happened within the Physical Plane.

The energy that reaches the Causal Plane develops a greater vibrational frequency. The increase in frequency results in conscious energy journeying to the Akashic Plane. It becomes part of the universal information at this dimension. However, there still remains a differentiation between past and future events at this level.

At the next level, the Mental Plane, conscious energy lacks any context of past or future. At this level, all informational content is experienced as being in the present moment. As it moves up further through the planes of consciousness, the conscious energy reaches the Messianic Plane, where the consciousness is further refined. At this level, there is only oneness of consciousness.

While the Mental Plane only contains information within the context of the present moment, even the concept of a present moment does not exist at the level of the Messianic Plane. At this level, there is only oneness. In oneness, concepts such as past, present, and future do not exist. With the dissolving of time and separation, conscious energy journeys on to the highest level of consciousness, the Heavenly Plane. When the conscious energy reaches the Heavenly Plane, it becomes pure energy. Pure energy is the same as pure consciousness. It is energy or consciousness that contains nothing but its own essence.

The Seven Planes of Existence provide a model to the nature of consciousness, from its most gross and conceptual level (the Physical Plane) to a level where it is just pure awareness (the Heavenly Plane). The entire universe is found within this model. By raising their vibrational frequency, mediums can access these higher planes. The spirits that they connect with are found in these higher planes. However, the medium, the spirits, and the various planes are one and the same. They are all aspects of consciousness. The only thing that separates them is their frequency level. They are different expressions of the same thing, and that thing is consciousness.

Those of us who are not mediums, and are unaware of our psychic powers, are part of this model. From a higher perspective, what mediums do is no different than anyone else. They communicate with others. However, the medium's reach is more expansive because they have raised their frequency. The next chapter will explore this at a deeper level.

Chapter 5: The Vibrational Frequency of Your Life

In this chapter, we will examine how thoughts, emotions, and chakras influence your vibrational frequency. We will begin with thoughts.

Thoughts: The Sculptors of Your Reality

Like everything else in this universe, thoughts are energy forms. You do not have thoughts. Instead, you attract thoughts that match your vibrational frequency. What we refer to as thoughts are bits of information from the Akashic Records. The Akashic Records are part of the nonphysical planes that comprise consciousness. Every thought that ever existed is found there.

Your vibrational frequency determines what thoughts you will attract from the Akashic Records. In turn, your vibrational frequency is determined by your level of consciousness. The more that you identify with your mind and body, the lower your vibrational frequency will be. To identify with the mind is to believe that who you are is what you think. In truth, thoughts lack any inherent power or meaning of their own. It is we who give thoughts their meaning and power. We give thoughts meaning and power when we identify with them or personalize them.

There are innumerable thoughts that travel through the field of consciousness, and most of them do not even register in your awareness. However, certain thoughts attract the attention of awareness. That which determines the level of interest in any given thought is the result of past karma.

In our manifested form, there are thoughts that our attention (which is awareness directed at an object) becomes attached to. Our attention energizes the thought, and then we project meaning onto it. This is what determines whether or not we identify with the thought. We define ourselves by the thoughts that we become attached to. In turn, these thoughts elicit behaviors from us. These behaviors reinforce the meaning that we give to the thought and what results from this are our habits.

The essence of our life is eternal; however, our manifested selves are ephemeral. While we may cease to exist in our physical form when we pass away, the psychic energy of thoughts will remain with the spirit. When the conditions are right, this psychic energy will occupy the life of someone who has a similar vibrational frequency as we did before our passing. This process is known as karma.

To give a personal example of how karma affects us, I have always had a great affinity for the ocean. That love that I felt for the ocean was just a form of energy that had become associated with the ocean during one of my previous lives. Because of my vibrational frequency, I attracted this karmic energy.

This karma remained latent within me until I saw the ocean for the first time in my life when I was three years old. It was then that my karma became activated. In my example of personal karma, I did not confuse the ocean as being me, for my mind treated the ocean as an object that existed outside of myself. What would happen if the object of my attention was not as clearly distinguishable?

Our beliefs (which are a form of thought) inform us of potential pleasure and potential pain. As a child, I had a parent who frequently criticized me. I had memories (a form of thought that I had given meaning to) when my parents disapproved of me. From the perspective of higher consciousness, there are no mistakes or accidents. However, my manifested form and that of my parents inhabited a lower plane of consciousness. When I made a "mistake", my memories reminded me of what happened in the past, which was disapproval.

My vibrational frequency dropped to the low range of the hierarchy. This drop in vibrational frequency resulted in me attracting other thoughts that matched my frequency. In other words, I attracted additional disempowering thoughts. It was through these accumulated thoughts that I experienced myself and the world around me.

When our manifested form identifies with a thought, we take on the persona of that thought. As with countless others, I mistook who I was for the thought-form that I gave importance to. The thought that I gave importance to was: "I cannot do anything right." For many years, this was my sense of identity. At some level, we all do this. Who we take ourselves to be is based on our conditioning, the conditioning that comes from society's indoctrination. As a society, we have yet to evolve to higher levels of consciousness. Unbeknownst to us, by accepting such indoctrination, we perpetuate our lower vibrational frequency by attracting lower vibrational thoughts.

Emotions and Their Energy Levels

It has been stated many times in this book that we identify with our mind and body. When we experience an emotion, we believe that it is OUR emotion that we are experiencing. The emotion that we are experiencing can be positive, neutral, or negative. This perspective of emotions is typical as it is the result of our ego-based mind. The ego-based mind quantifies, classifies, and personalizes our experience of reality. From the perspective of higher levels of consciousness, reality is seamless. There is no distinction or separation in our experiences. Everything that we experience blends together to form a seamless experience.

At higher levels of consciousness, there is no happiness, sadness, fear, or joy. These are just labels that our minds create. Further, the emotions that you feel do not belong to you. As stated before, the basis for all of existence is energy. When we experience an emotion, we are experiencing energy that appears at different vibratory frequencies. When we experience energy with a high frequency, we call it "happiness" or "love." If low-frequency energy is experienced, we call it "apathy," "fear," or anger."

Each of us is an energetic entity within a larger energy field. Just as a wave is a modification of the ocean's surface, we modify the larger energy field. The vibrational frequency of your energy field is determined by how freely energy can flow. When we are not conscious of our energy levels, we become vulnerable to the influence of other energy fields.

Have you ever been in the company of someone who left you feeling drained just by being around them? The experience of feeling drained results from you allowing their weak energy to enter your energy field, which led to the lowering of yours. In this book, you will learn how to maintain your energy level and strengthen it to take your life to the next level!

I remember attending my father's funeral. My acceptance of his passing, along with my spiritual understanding of death, allowed me to be at peace. All that changed when each guest was invited to speak of their memories of him. When my sister spoke, she broke down in tears. Spontaneously, I did the same, though I did not feel sadness.

Through the years of conditioning, my body responded to my sister's energetic field as though it was my own. We are constantly taking on the energies of others, which then influences ours. We then mistakenly, but understandably, claim that the emotion that we are experiencing is our own.

As you learn to raise your energy level, you will become more vigilant of the vibrational fields of others. You will more likely be able to maintain your vibrational frequency. Having this ability will also benefit you in becoming more successful in demonstrating your psychic powers.

As stated earlier, each emotion is part of an energetic continuum and can be classified according to its frequency level. The following is a more detailed explanation of the hierarchy of emotions:

Apathy: Apathy is ranked as the lowest of the emotions on the list because all emotional connection is cut off when we are experiencing apathy. Apathy is a condition where emotions are suppressed. Since emotions are energy, apathy is the suppression of energy.

Shame: The emotion of shame is the second-lowest emotion as it involves negatively focusing on yourself. Since you are energizing the low-frequency thoughts you have of yourself, you attract other thoughts of the same frequency.

Guilt: Guilt is the next lowest emotion. The emotion of guilt is intended to message you that you need to change your beliefs about your relationship with other people. If you change your beliefs for more empowering ones, then guilt has performed its function. If you dwell on how inadequate you are as a human being, you have thrown yourself to the mercy of the mind. While shame is based on self-worth, guilt is more based on behavior.

Grief: Grief is the emotion of loss, and the sense of loss is based on a sense of separation. From the point of higher levels of consciousness, it is impossible to experience grief because the sense of separation does not exist.

Fear: While grief is the emotion of loss, fear is the anticipation of loss. The emotion of fear comes from experiencing ourselves as a separate entity from the rest of life. By feeling separate, we become attached to the world of form. Our sense of security is threatened whenever the world of form does not meet our expectations. This dynamic is vividly seen in relationships. We feel insecure in our relationships when our partner does not live up to our expectations. When this happens, our sense of security is shaken. It happens because we have based our sense of self on the world of form rather than our eternal aspect.

Anger: Anger is a reaction to fear, and it has a higher frequency than fear. We experience anger because we feel something that we have identified with is being threatened. If you did not feel identified with that which is being threatened, you would not become angry. You would not feel angry if someone rear-ended another driver. However, you would likely experience anger if the rear-ended car were yours.

Satisfaction: The emotion of satisfaction is a higher vibration than anger because it involves less identification. Both anger and fear are experienced as the result of identifying with something outside ourselves. The emotion of satisfaction is an indicator that the emotion of fear is temporarily absent. While being of a higher frequency than anger, the emotion of satisfaction will be fleeting as long as we continue to identify with our thoughts or the people and objects around us.

Happiness: The emotion of happiness is of a higher frequency than the emotion of satisfaction. However, the happiness that most of us experience is dependent on the conditions of our life being to our liking, which is a challenge given that everything in the phenomenal world changes. To seek out relationships for the purpose of becoming happy is like building sandcastles on the ocean's edge; it will remain standing only until the next wave.

Joy: Joy is the emotion that we experience when that which we deeply desire is realized in our lives. Joy is a higher vibration than happiness; however, it is an unstable emotion if the source of joy is found outside us.

Gratitude: Gratitude is a higher-vibratory level than joy because it involves acknowledging others for what they add to our lives. The challenge with gratitude occurs when it is only experienced upon receiving something tangible. When this happens, our experience of it will be at the mercy of external conditions.

Appreciation: Appreciation is a higher frequency than gratitude because the emotion of appreciation can be experienced independently of whether or not we receive something. In other words, we can appreciate something for just being itself. For example, we can have an appreciation for a beautiful sunset or the work of an artist.

Love: We frequently think of love as being the most powerful force in the universe, which is true if that love is unconditional. Since the love that we experience is normally conditional, it is subject to change as our external conditions change. An example of this would be when our partner does not meet our expectations.

Enlightenment: Enlightenment has the highest vibratory level of any energy. Unconditional love can be equated with enlightenment; however, enlightenment can be achieved without first developing unconditional love, which is extremely rare. A more practical approach to enlightenment can be achieved by practicing meditation and self-inquiry.

These practices can lead to the expansion of awareness, where we realize that who we are is beyond our mind and body. However, this awareness must be achieved through direct experience; it cannot be achieved intellectually or by reading about it.

You may have noticed a pattern with the hierarchy of emotions. The higher one goes up the hierarchy, the less one is influenced by external factors. Conversely, the lower we go on the hierarchy, the more reactive we become toward external factors.

From the higher perspective of higher consciousness, external factors are not exclusively what appear in the world around us. It also includes our "inner world," which includes mental phenomena such as thoughts and emotions.

In the last two sections, we covered how thoughts and emotions play a role in energy flow. In the next section, we will explore how our bodies affect our vibrational frequency.

The Body as an Energy Field

Before launching into this section of the book, I want you to try a simple experiment:

1. Sit down and make yourself comfortable.
2. Now turn your hands so that your palms are facing each other. Keep your hands relaxed.
3. Next, slowly bring your hands together without touching and then slowly pull them away. As you pull them away, make sure that your palms remain facing each other.
4. As you do this, do you feel anything? What you are feeling is your body's energy.
5. If you do not feel anything, keep practicing this exercise until you do.

The ability to feel your body's energy is not limited to your palms. Your entire body is an energy field; however, detecting that energy is easier in some areas of the body than others. For most people, the palms are one of those areas where energy detection is easily experienced.

Within the body-energy field are energy centers known as chakras. The study of chakras can be traced back to Buddhist and Hindu traditions. The word "chakra" is a Sanskrit word whose English translation means "wheel." Found throughout the body, these "wheels" of energy are located near the major nerve centers of the body and regulate the flow of energy.

The seven main chakras in the body are the root chakra, sacral chakra, solar plexus, heart chakra, throat chakra, third eye chakra, and the crown chakra. The seven chakras create a network; hence, they are interconnected. What happens in one chakra can affect all the other chakras.

The seven chakras are continuously changing regarding their ability to regulate the flow of energy. An analogy of this is a car's engine. Fuel enters the engine. Each of the engine's various components interacts with the fuel in a specific way that eventually allows the engine to run.

If any of the engine's components are not functioning properly, there will be problems with the car's performance. If not corrected, other engine components can become affected as well. As you will soon see, each of the seven chakras is specialized in the role that they play in regulating the flow of energy. For example, the root chakra is associated with a sense of stability and security. In contrast, the sacral chakra is associated with creativity and sexuality.

Our sense of wellbeing, physically and emotionally, is dependent on whether our chakras are balanced with each other. Besides being associated with various parts of the body, each chakra is associated with a specific element and color. Elements include the various earth elements and psychological ones. At the same time, color provides a reference to any given chakra when meditating, which will be discussed in a later chapter. With a basic understanding of chakras, you can learn how to maintain your chakras so that your energy flows properly. In turn, properly flowing energy leads to physical and emotional wellbeing as a result of raising your vibrational frequency.

The following is an overview of the seven chakras:

Root Chakra (also known as Muladhara)

The root chakra is:

- Associated with one's sense of emotional stability and security, as well as one's basic needs. When this chakra is open, we feel calm and confident. When blocked, we experience fear, anxiety, or doubt.
- Located near the lower spine.
- Associated with the color red.
- Associated with the Earth element.

The Sacral Chakra (also known as Svadhishthana)

The sacral chakra is:

- Associated with one's sense of creativity, sexuality, and ability to adapt to new situations. When we doubt our creative potential or experience anxiety over any aspect of our sexuality, we create an imbalance in this chakra.
- Located approximately two inches below the navel.
- Associated with the color orange.
- Associated with the element of Water.

The Solar Plexus Chakra (also known as Manipura)

The Solar Plexus Chakra is:

- Associated with our sense of autonomy, self-esteem, and determination. When balanced, the solar plexus chakra leads to clarifying how to move forward with one's goal. For this reason, this chakra is important if we are to achieve success in our pursuits. Conversely, this chakra can become unbalanced if we focus on our perceived failures in life. Having low self-esteem is caused by the blockage of this chakra.

- Located in the upper abdomen, just below the center of the ribs.
- Associated with the color yellow.
- Associated with the element of Fire.

The Heart Chakra (also known as Anahata)

The heart chakra is associated with our ability to experience love and compassion. It is the most powerful of the energy centers. Emotions are energy forms, and they have a hierarchy as each one relates to their vibrational frequency. Fear has the lowest frequency, while love and compassion are on top of the spectrum. These emotions are on top because they reflect the qualities of our essential nature, which are oneness and wholeness. The energy of love and compassion dissolves the mind's illusions of separation and our egocentric tendencies. The heart chakra unites the mind, body, and soul, resulting in the sense of inner peace. The heart chakra becomes balanced when the happiness of others becomes our focal point, and we experience compassion and empathy for what they may be going through. There are various popular sayings about love, such as:

- Love conquers all.
- All that you need is love.
- Love makes the world go around.

- Love is the answer.

These sayings are more than just "feel good" adages. They depict a timeless, though possibly subconscious, understanding of love's power. Love is more than just a sentiment, for its energy is the energy of creation. Love is the substratum for all of existence; it is made experiential to us in the form of a feeling.

The illusions of the mind create a sense of separation within us, which creates an ego-centered mind. From such a mind, fear, a sense of scarcity, and a lack of compassion and empathy are given birth. The energy of love dissolves the ego-centered mind. It reminds us of our higher nature, which is the energy of love. If you did nothing else but opened your heart chakra, you would regain balance in the remaining energy centers.

What causes the heart chakra to close are any negative perceptions that we hold regarding love— be it a failed relationship, the loss of a loved one, or the experience of heartbreak. From the level of everyday consciousness, such events create a sense of pain and loss within us. From the perspective of higher consciousness, pain and loss do not exist, for love is eternal.

The Heart Chakra is:
- Located in the area of the heart.
- Associated with the color green.
- Associated with the element of air.

The Throat Chakra (also known as Vishuddha)

The throat chakra provides a passage for energy from the lower body to the head. It is associated with our ability for self-expression through sound. The voice is our original instrument for communication, predating the written word. More than just sound, the energy from the throat chakra reveals the heart's desires, which speak more loudly than words alone.

This energy center is why the words of others sometimes deeply resonate with us and reach us at the deepest level. The Sanskrit word "Vishubba" means "pure" or "purification."

When we speak with directness and honesty, our words are filled with the energy of the throat chakra. When the throat chakra is balanced, one speaks from the heart and is understood by others. The communication of such a one is forthright yet respectful of others.

Imbalances of the throat chakra occur when the ego-based mind attempts to take charge of communication to prove others wrong or prove itself worthy. Anytime the motive of our words is to justify who we are, we have removed ourselves from the throat chakra's energy. When the throat chakra is blocked, we have difficulty communicating what we want to say. We also may believe that others are not interested in what we have to say.

The throat chakra is:

- Located in the throat area.
- Associated with the color blue.
- Associated with the element of air.

The Third-Eye Chakra (also known as Ajana)

As our level of consciousness rises, we experience things that we did not experience at the lower levels. Phenomena such as intuition, spiritual contemplation, self-reflection, extrasensory perception, and visions of past lives are just a few examples of this. The potential for us to experience these things has always been there; we did not have the awareness to experience them.

The energy center that makes metaphysical experiences possible is the third-eye chakra. The Sanskrit word "Ajna" can be translated as "to perceive or to command." When your third eye is balanced, you are able to receive intuition. Accordingly, you will take action, even when there is nothing to validate the way you feel. Those whose third eye is open are effective as mediums.

When one learns to use the third-eye chakra, one transcends the ego-based mind and can view all of reality with non-judgment and acceptance. In other words, one becomes a silent witness to all that is. This witnessing is not just of the outer world but the inner world as well. Such a person can observe their thoughts without becoming entangled in them or personalizing them. For this reason, there is clarity of thought. What causes the third eye to become unbalanced is the doubting of one's intuition due to the influence of others and relying too much on the rational mind.

The third-eye chakra is:
- Located in the center of the brow.
- Associated with the color indigo.
- Associated with the element of light.

The Crown Chakra (also known as Sahasrara)

Along with the heart chakra, the crown chakra is one of the most important energy centers. The crown chakra determines the level of our spiritual alignment. The experience of inner peace, and the ability to communicate with the higher conscious realms, is heavily influenced by the crown chakra. Other spiritual benefits include a deep appreciation for beauty and the feeling of joy.

When the crown chakra is balanced, it serves as a conduit to our highest self. We are multidimensional beings. We simultaneously inhabit the non-phenomenal realm of higher consciousness and the physical dimension of this Earthly plane. When the crown chakra is balanced, we are aligned with the higher aspect of ourselves. When it is unbalanced, it leads to self-doubt and a sense of lack of purpose.

The crown chakra is:

- Located on the top of the head.
- Associated with the color violet.
- Associated with the element of thought.

In this section, we covered the energy centers of the body. In the next section, we will explore in greater detail what causes the energy centers to be balanced or not.

The Mind, Body, and your Vibrational Frequency

The balance of the seven chakras is important to physical and mental wellbeing. Unbalanced chakras cause us to attract low vibrational thoughts and emotions. The hierarchy of emotions that was previously discussed is ordered by the vibrational quality of each emotion. When we personalize low vibrational emotions, we create an unbalanced chakra system.

An unbalanced chakra system makes it difficult to connect with higher dimensions of consciousness. This is due to us identifying with these low-level emotions. By identifying with these low-level emotions, we attract other emotions of similar quality. When this happens, it reinforces our belief that these emotions are who we are.

Those higher emotions, such as gratitude, appreciation, and love, are at the upper end of the vibrational hierarchy. Because of their higher vibrational frequency, they are in alignment with the higher dimensions of consciousness. These emotions cause us to shift our attention from the ego-based mind to other individuals or nature. Since our attention is no longer monopolized by the ego-based mind, our energetic life force increases in frequency.

The concern for others is what defeats the ego-based mind and allows us to open up to the spiritual realm. Our chakras maintain the circulation of this high-frequency energy, allowing us to access the spiritual realm and raise our vibrational frequency even further.

Our thoughts and emotions play a vital role in gaining us access to our higher selves. In fact, thoughts and emotions are two sides of the same coin. Emotions are energy forms that operate like a GPS in a car. The GPS of a car provides information to the driver on how to reach their desired destination. Emotions provide us with information about whether a given situation will lead to potential pain or potential pleasure.

If you become angry about a situation, it is because you believe that the situation will lead you to experience pain. If you are joyful, you believe that the situation will lead to a pleasurable experience. Beliefs, which are a form of thought, serve us in a similar manner. If you believe that people are only out for themselves and take advantage of you if given a chance, you will behave accordingly to avoid a painful experience.

On the other hand, if you believe people are good, that belief will determine your behavior when dealing with others. You will view interacting with others as a source of pleasure. What is important to note is that our beliefs are purely subjective and do not reflect true reality. Rather, our beliefs create our reality.

The quality of our thoughts will lead to the experiencing of emotions that are of like kind. If I have a negative thought, then I will experience a negative emotion. Suppose I change my thinking and start thinking empowering thoughts. In that case, my emotions will be positive, which will lead to an increase in my vibrational level.

It is important to note that all thoughts and emotions have their place. Raising your vibrational level has nothing to do with denying how you feel. Rather, it is about learning to accept all of your thoughts and emotions but not becoming attached to them. By accepting your thoughts and emotions, you provide the openness for your attention to be redirected toward something that will empower you. If I am feeling sorry for myself, I can allow myself to experience these feelings while at the same time looking at what I can appreciate or be grateful for in my life.

That our thoughts and emotions mirror each other as it relates to their informational content is a gift from the universe. We all have subconscious thoughts that we are not aware of. Thoughts become subconscious when we continuously deny their existence. Though we may not be aware of our subconscious thoughts, we can learn to gain access to them if we try to understand the emotions that we are experiencing. When we can bring our subconscious thoughts to the light, we will have taken an important step to raise our vibrational frequency and balance our chakras.

Chapter 6: Discovering Your Psychic Ability

As stated before, all of us have psychic abilities. However, most of us are unaware of it. This chapter will explore what prevents us from recognizing our psychic abilities and how we can strengthen them.

Your Daily Psychic Experiences

One of the major challenges that we have that prevents us from recognizing our psychic experiences is that we attribute them to something else or dismiss them as insignificant. Take a look at this list and see if you can relate to any of these:

- You feel like someone is looking at you.
- Out of the blue, you think of someone, only to have them show up or call you later.
- You enter a room and get a bad feeling about it.
- You enter a room and get a good feeling about it.
- You see someone who you do not know and get a bad feeling about them.

- You see someone who you do not know and get a good feeling about them.
- You get a feeling that someone you know is upset or needs help, only to confirm this when you follow up with them later on.
- You are taking a shower, taking it easy, or doing some other relaxing activity, and out of nowhere you get some insight about something.

This list is just a few examples that may signify that you are experiencing your psychic powers. Psychic powers can allow you to receive information in a manner that is unexplainable by science or established knowledge. However, such abilities are found throughout the natural world. There are bird species that migrate vast distances to return to their nesting grounds. Sea turtles do the same thing, even though they had never made the trip before! As a personal anecdote, my dog knows what my intentions are before I even act on them. I once was going to give him a bath, and he took off running!

Another thing that is important to understand about psychic powers is that there is great variability in how we experience them. In this book, we have discussed a range of psychic powers by breaking them up into different topics. An example of this would be the four clairs: clairvoyance, clairsentience, clairaudience, and claircognizance. It is not the case that one person has clairvoyance only while another may only have clairaudience. A person may have a mixture of the different clairs, though some of those clairs may be better developed than others.

In this book, the various psychic powers were clearly delineated; however, these clear distinctions often become less clear when they are experienced. Rather than getting caught up in the various terminologies and descriptions, it is more important to realize that you can receive information mentally that may not be explainable. To become a medium, you just need to cultivate these abilities to more fully experience them and gain greater confidence in your abilities.

Learning to Tune to Your Channel

Learning to access your psychic powers is similar to tuning in a radio station. When tuning in a radio station, you will receive static unless you are right on the station. Similarly, you will receive static when you first start off trying to tune your psychic powers. You may experience things that may not seem relevant; however, do not ignore them. Be willing to receive everything that you experience without judgment. Do so with even seemingly negative thoughts or emotions. Make yourself open to everything. You want to invite everything that enters your experience. Trust that there is a reason for this to be happening and that you will be safe. The more you practice, the more familiar that you will become with your psychic powers.

Additionally, it is important to have fun as you learn to access your psychic powers. If you treat it too seriously, you will not experience the openness needed to experience them.

If you think of the times when you experienced your intuition, most likely it occurred when you were relaxed and not caught up in your thoughts. Your intuition is one of your most basic psychic powers. In fact, all psychic powers are expressions of your intuition. It is for this reason that it is important to learn how to trust yourself. For you to trust yourself also means to learn to trust your intuition.

To maximize your abilities to experience your psychic powers, have fun practicing and approach it with curiosity. As you go through your day, take time to practice your psychic powers by listening to your intuition and following up with it. You then can determine the validity of the message that you received. For example, let us say you are relaxing when you think that a friend of yours is having a bad day. Call your friend and ask them how their day was. See if your intuition was correct or not.

Remember; make a game out of it. If you find out that you were correct, get excited but do not make more out of it than it is. It is important to keep practicing to prove that it was not just a coincidence that you were right in your predictions.

In the same manner, do not judge yourself if your intuition does not pan out. This does not mean that you were wrong. Think about the radio metaphor, the static is not what you want to hear, but it is real. Similarly, suppose you get intuitive moments that you are unable to substantiate. In that case, it does not mean the message you received was wrong. These messages do have relevance, though they may not be understood at the present time.

It is also important to know that your intuitive insights will come in waves. At times, you will not receive anything. This is normal; do not try to force it. Insights will usually come to you when you are feeling relaxed.

Psychic Powers and Imagination

It is important to realize that the thing that is preventing you from fully experiencing your psychic powers is your rational mind. Our rational mind is the filter through which most of us experience life. Your rational mind is filled with concepts and information you have learned since you were just a baby.

While thoughts are part of the rational mind, psychic abilities are not part of it. It is for this reason that most of us are unaware of our psychic abilities. Your thoughts do not leave an opening for your psychic powers to get through. When your mind is relaxed, then your psychic abilities have an opportunity to reach you. The problem is that when you experience your intuition, you allow your rational mind to determine the meaning of your experience. Your rational mind will tell you things like:

- It's nothing; it is just your imagination.
- Ignore it; it does not mean anything.
- It was just a coincidence that things happened that way.

A common question among those who are learning to develop their intuitive abilities is how you distinguish between intuition and your thoughts. Thoughts will have an emotional connection to them. For example, if you think that a certain person should not be trusted, you will experience emotions with that thought. Perhaps you will feel fear or concern. In contrast, intuition is information that is not accompanied by emotions.

If you want to clear your rational mind and leave room for your intuition to break through, one way is to allow your imagination to run free. Take time during your day where you allow yourself to just daydream. The more you allow yourself to explore your imagination, the more likely you will receive information from your intuition.

Trust and Verify

Whenever you experience your intuition, do not dismiss it. Trust it as being a message from higher levels of consciousness. At the same time, seek to verify if the message is valid or not. For example, if you get the message that someone you know is having a bad day, follow up with them and ask them how their day went.

If you find out that your intuition was not correct, do not judge yourself or doubt the message. Verification is an important aspect in strengthening your intuitive abilities. After repeatedly verifying the messages you receive, you will learn to recognize the difference between your intuition and your mind playing games with you.

Do not be afraid to be wrong. Learning to develop your psychic abilities is a process. This process needs to be repeated to refine your ability to distinguish between a psychic message and your mind running wild. For this to happen, you need to be open to all information that you receive.

Ways to Trust Your Intuition

The following are ways for you to learn to develop confidence in your intuition:

Say It and Do It

When you get a message from your intuition, announce it out loud (you may want to do this when you are alone) and then take action on the message that you receive. If your intuition tells you to go someplace, say it out loud and go to that place, if possible. Start off with low consequential messages, meaning that you will not experience any meaningful consequences if things do not go as planned. As you gain confidence in your ability, you can then apply this technique to messages that are consequential to you. By confidently announcing your message and taking action on it, you will develop your ability to recognize and trust your intuition.

Write It Down

Make it a daily habit to write down what your intuition tells you. Record it in a journal. Also, record your dreams and any feelings or visions that may be revealed to you. Additionally, record how you experienced the messages that you received. Were they in the form of intuition or a feeling? Were they in the form of a vision or in a dream? By recording your experiences, you can look for patterns. You can track your predictions and determine if there are any reoccurring, which ones eventually became true and how you received the messages (Intuitively, through vision, or through feeling).

Ask for a Sign

Another way to gain confidence in your intuition is to ask for a sign. Ask the universe for a sign that will confirm the validity of the message that you received.

Practice Reading Energy

An easy way to practice your psychic skills is to read other people's energy. Experience their energy and then follow up with them to see if you can verify your prediction. To do this, relax your mind and place yourself in their presence. When reading their energy, you do not want to be influenced by their physical appearance or body language. You want to do this before you start interacting with them. After experiencing their energy, initiate a conversation with them to see if you can verify your prediction.

Remote Viewing

Remote viewing is an example of clairvoyance. In remote viewing, one can view faraway places. When remote viewing, it is important to first relax and quiet your mind. Next, think about a place that you are unfamiliar with. See if you get any visions of this place. For example, I had plans to go to a store the next day; it was a store that I had never been to before. That night, I thought about the store and asked for information about it. Various visions came to me of different aspects of the store. I saw the kind of floor it had and some objects that were on the shelves. The next day, I went to the store and was pleased to find that my visions of the store were accurate.

Contact Your Sprit Guides

To contact your spirit guides, ask for a specific sign that is unordinary. For example, let us say you want verification that making a career change is the right move for you. Ask the universe for a sign by showing you a purple shoe. This example demonstrates the importance of asking for a specific sign that is unordinary. If your sign appears, you will know that it was due to your asking.

Abandon Your Resentment

To realize your psychic ability, you need to come to peace with all those around you. This does not mean that you pretend that what happened in the past does not matter. What it means that you learn to forgive those around you with whom you have differences. In forgiving them, you are actually healing yourself by no longer holding on to your resentment toward them. Resentment is a killer of psychic powers.

Use Your Psychic Powers for Good

Your intentions for developing your psychic powers should be to create value for your life and others. More powerfully, you should strive to use your psychic abilities for the benefit of others. To use your psychic powers for self-serving reasons, at the expense of others, is a sure way for you to lose connection with your psychic abilities.

You Must Be Brave

When you start practicing your psychic abilities, you are almost certain to experience things that may scare you. Your fear of experiencing something scary is sure to keep you from accessing your psychic abilities. There is nothing that you can experience from the supernatural realm that can harm you. You need to have the attitude of complete acceptance for whatever should arise. As long as you do not react to it, you will be fine.

Practice Psychometrics

Psychometrics is the ability to receive information about the past by touching objects. You can practice this by touching an object until you experience its energy. When connected with its energy, try to get information about the object's history or its owner. As with all exercises for developing your psychic skills, approach it playfully. Do not get disappointed if nothing happens. It takes time and practice to develop your skills.

Practice Telepathy

Telepathy is the ability to communicate thoughts with others without words or gestures. You can practice this by having someone pick a number or draw a card from a deck and then predicting what they selected. Another technique is to have them draw something, and then you identify it. Developing telepathy takes daily practice for years; however, you will improve as time goes on.

In this chapter, you learned about ways to develop your psychic abilities. Regardless of what method you use, there is a foundational area of your life that you need to address. Your beliefs are the most important factor as to whether you are successful in developing your psychic potential. If you have limiting beliefs about your abilities, you will struggle to develop your psychic powers. In the next chapter, you will learn how to change any thoughts limiting your beliefs and replace them with empowering ones.

Chapter 7: How to Change your Beliefs

If you want to develop your psychic abilities, you need to have the mentality that there is no place for self-doubt. You will need to trust your abilities. This chapter will explore ways to change any beliefs that you may have that create doubt within you. By identifying the beliefs that are creating doubt in your life, you will bring them to the light of your awareness. This will reduce the potency of these beliefs. You can then develop new and more empowering beliefs to take their place. The very process of identifying your disempowering beliefs and adopting empowering ones is an act of self-love.

The Ultimate Why

With sincere reflection, most of us can determine why we do what we do; however, the answer is usually just a surface answer. If you really want to get to the root cause of what drives your behavior, you need to reveal your "ultimate why," which is often found at the subconscious level. Your "ultimate why" is the real reason you engage in the thinking or behaviors that prevent you from going forward to achieve your goals, including the development of your psychic powers.

Before you start the exercise, take time to write down those aspects of your life that are bothering you. When you make your list, it is important to be brutally honest with yourself. Do not hold anything back. When you have made your list, determine which of these items impact you the most from experiencing your psychic powers.

You will be using this item for the following exercise. To explain how to do this exercise, I will use an example to see how the process works. The item from my list that I chose was: "I have a hard time believing that I have psychic powers."

1. I would then ask myself, "What does it mean to me to doubt that I have psychic powers?"
    My answer would be, "It means that I do not want to seem gullible or unrealistic."
2. I would then ask myself, "What would it mean to me to be gullible or unrealistic?"
    I would respond by saying, "It means that I do not want to be foolish."
3. I would then ask, "What would it mean to me if I was being foolish?"
    I would respond, "It would mean that I would be judged by others."
4. I would then ask, "What would it mean to me to be judged by others?"
    I would respond with, "It means that I was not good enough."

5. I would then ask, "What would it mean to me if I was not good enough?"
   I would respond with, "It means that no one will ever love me."

The belief that "No one will ever love me" is the root cause. It is the root belief that is causing me to doubt my psychic powers. If I lived in a society that encouraged people to develop their psychic powers, I would feel motivated to develop my psychic abilities.

Without identifying the root belief, I would continue to doubt my psychic abilities. Further, this belief would reduce my vibrational level; thus, preventing me from experiencing my psychic powers.

Turning the Tables on a Root Belief

Now that you have identified your root belief, your next step is to reprogram your brain by identifying with all the pain that your root belief has caused you in the past. You will then reflect on all the benefits you would gain by replacing it with an empowering belief. To do this exercise, do the following:

1. Get two sheets of paper. Select paper sizes of 8" x 11" or larger.
2. Take the first sheet of paper and fold it in half lengthwise.
3. On the top of the paper, write down your root belief.
4. On the left-hand side of the paper, make a list of how this belief has cost you in the past. Think of how this root belief has affected you in all your life areas. Ask

yourself how this belief has affected you in how you see yourself, how it has affected your emotional health, your relationships, your physical health, your work, your finances, and so on.

5. When writing, keep in mind the following:

    - When writing this list, write down the first thing that comes to your mind, even if it seems irrelevant.

    - Write as fast as you can and feel the emotions that arise. This is a heartfelt exercise, not a thinking one.

    - Keep writing until you run out of things to write.

6. By each item that you write down, assign an arbitrary point value as to how much impact this item has had on you. When selecting the point value, choose the first number that comes to mind.

7. When you have completed assigning the point values, find the total of all the point values and place it at the bottom of the page.

8. For the right side of the page, repeat steps 6-7, except this time, you will write down all the ways this belief has benefited you.

When you have completed Step 8, think of a new alternative belief that empowers you. For example, if the original belief was "No one will ever love me," my new belief may be, "The only love that I can depend on is the love that I give to myself."

On the second piece of paper, and using your new belief, repeat steps 1-8 but reverse Steps 6 and 8. For Steps 6, write down all the ways you believe you would benefit from this new belief. For Step 8, write down all the ways you believe it will cost you.

When you have completed the two sheets, do the following:
1. Immediately review your lists, allowing yourself to fully experience any emotions that arise.
2. Review your lists every day, once in the morning and once before you go to bed, until you become fully associated with the emotions that you experience.

When you become fully associated with the costs of holding on to your old belief with the benefits of adopting your new belief, your mind will become programmed with your new belief. Besides changing your beliefs, it is also important to give up any resistance you have toward yourself or your life. As a matter of fact, if you give up your resistance, you will automatically eliminate your limiting beliefs. We will learn how to do so in the next section.

When Thoughts and Emotions Celebrate

When I was much younger, I was at a New Year's celebration with my family. Just before the clock struck midnight, I saw someone grab a bottle of champagne, shake it up, and remove the cork. The champagne erupted like a geyser as it shot out of the bottle, soaking all those who were around. This event is a good metaphor for the subconscious and its impact on our ability to experience our psychic powers. In the case of the champagne, its behavior was the result of pressure being released. The champagne's bubbles result from the buildup of carbon dioxide, which creates pressure because the cork prevents its escape. Removing the cork allows the pressure to be released.

Our subconscious thoughts and emotions are like champagne bubbles. As indicated earlier, emotions mirror thought. The reason for this is that emotions and thoughts are not separate entities. If you are experiencing negative emotions, it is because you are giving attention to negative thoughts. Both of these mental phenomena are the same energy experienced in different ways.

Thoughts are recognized for their apparent linguistic quality, meaning that they seem to be talking to us. We mistake this "voice" to be our "minds." Emotions are experienced as sensations that we feel. The subconsciousness is like the champagne bottle, and the cork is like resistance. What do I mean by resistance? Resistance is what happens whenever we do not accept or deny what we are experiencing. When we experience a thought or emotions that are too painful for us, we withdraw our attention from it, which is a form of resistance. When this repeatedly occurs, these thoughts and emotions eventually become suppressed.

The First Law of Thermodynamics states that energy cannot be created or destroyed. It can only take on a different form. What this means is that when we suppress a thought, it does not just go away. Instead, it takes on a different form of energy. This suppressed energy is what causes the body's energy centers to become imbalanced. Further, it prevents us from experiencing our psychic powers. Why is that? To understand this, we first need to return to consciousness.

As manifested beings, we are the ones that experience the world. The experience that we place our attention on is what informs the conscious energy system. When we resist experiencing a thought or emotion, our attention is focused on the act of resisting. If the consciousness energy system could speak, it would be saying: "Oh, you want more things to resist."

The consciousness energy system then manifests more things for us to resist. Since the whole process occurs at the subconscious level, we are not aware of it. When we try to bring forth our psychic powers that intention becomes canceled out by the resistance that we experience.

Additionally, our ability to experience our psychic powers is also compromised because creating resistance toward unpleasant thoughts or emotions consumes a great deal of energy. Negative emotional energy directly affects the body's chakras. All of this happens because we find some thoughts or emotions to be too painful to experience.

We can liberate ourselves from subconscious negative energies by learning to accept all of our experiences. Accepting that which you experience does not mean being cheerful of optimistic about life. Instead, it means acknowledging what is being experienced and not resisting it. Our thoughts and emotions are like little children. If you do not give them your attention, they will find a way to get it some other way, even if it means doing something negative. If we acknowledge our thoughts and emotions, they will not be driven into the depths of the subconscious. Instead, they will celebrate!

Now that you have read about the different emotions and subconscious thoughts, it is now time to put what you learned into practice. This next exercise will guide you toward transforming the negative energies in your subconscious by focusing on your feelings.

1. Sit down in a comfortable position and close your eyes.
2. Follow your breath during inhalation and exhalation. Place your attention on your breath; feel it as it courses through your body.
3. Now think about a situation that is concerning you. As you think of this situation, observe the emotions and sensations that arise from within you.
4. Now ask yourself, "Why does this situation bother me?" "What does this situation mean to me?" As you answer these questions, pay attention to the feelings that you are experiencing.
5. Now ask yourself, "That which I am experiencing, what does it feel like?" For example, you may be experiencing tension. Using this example, the next question you would ask yourself would be, "What does tension feel like?" Continuing with the example, I would say that tension feels constricted and heavy.

   Notice that the question was not what you think about tension; do not involve your thoughts in this process. Ask yourself, "What does it FEEL like?" Get in touch with what your experience FEELS like. Also, do not doubt yourself; go with the first answer that comes to you.

Do not worry about the words you use; focus on identifying the feeling. Make sure that you continue to breathe as you experience the feeling. Allow yourself to dive into it.

6. Whatever your response was to the last question, ask yourself, "What does that feel like?" Going back to the previous example, if tension feels like my body is constricted and heavy, the next question that I would ask myself is, "What does being constricted and heavy feel like?" Continuing with my example, I would say, "Being constricted and heavy feels like I am being crushed by a boulder." Whatever answer you receive, you would get in touch with its feeling. Making sure that you continue to breathe as you experience the feeling.

7. Whatever your response was to the last question, ask yourself, "What does that feel like?" If my response were that being constricted and heavy feels like I am being crushed by a boulder, I would then ask myself, "What does being crushed by a boulder feel like?"

8. The format for this meditation is to repeatedly ask yourself, "What does it feel like?" After asking the question, dive into the feeling and fully experience it. As always, continue to breathe.

9. When you continuously ask these questions, the feelings will transform on their own.

10. You will know you reached the end when the previously unpleasant feeling feels pleasant or neutral.

11. You can also use this same mediation on positive emotions, in which case, the positive feeling of the emotion will expand.

12. Repeat this meditation until you can successfully transform a negative emotion. Just for clarification, emotions are not positive or negative; they feel negative or positive by the meaning that we give them. For this reason, this meditation works; you are giving your emotions attention without imposing judgment on them.

Changing your limiting beliefs and releasing your resistance is important if one develops one's psychic ability. However, what if you are unaware of your limiting beliefs or resistance? In the next chapter, we will explore the concept of mindfulness. When you develop your ability to be mindful, you will be aware of all these things, including your psychic abilities.

Chapter 8: Mindfulness

What is Mindfulness?

There was a servant who had worked for years serving his master. The master lived in a large mansion but would never leave his room. Each morning, the servant would report to his master's room to get his instructions for the day. The door was always locked so that the servant would listen to his master's orders through the closed door.

One day, the servant performed his duties when he saw a maid who worked at the mansion. The servant shared with the maid how he was becoming more and more displeased with his master. "I have worked for my master for many years, and I do everything he asks me to do, yet he is never pleased. Nothing is ever good enough for him; he always wants more and more."

The maid told the servant that he should talk to the master about this and let him know how he felt. The servant thought about what the maid said. He had realized that he had always listened to the master without ever questioning him. He was so frustrated at this point that he decided that he would talk to his master.

The servant went to the master's door and called out his name, but there was no response. He then knocked on the door, still no response. The servant then turned the doorknob, and the door opened. The servant could not believe it; the door was unlocked. Never before had the door not been locked!

The servant gathered his courage and entered his master's room; what he saw left him stunned. His master's room was completely empty; there was no furniture or master! The servant stood in the empty room in despair, realizing that he had spent all these years serving someone who did not exist.

The story of the servant and his master illustrate the importance of practicing mindfulness, which is to become the master of our minds instead of our minds becoming the master of us. Similar to the locked room that contained an illusionary master, our minds always issue thoughts, which we frequently observe without questioning.

When the Mind Masters Us

When you take a shower in the morning, do you experience the sensations of water gliding across your flesh, or are you caught up in your thoughts? When you eat, do you savor the taste and texture of your food or do you just swallow it while being preoccupied with thought? When you walk outside, do you notice the delicate leaves of plants and how the sunlight enhances their color, or are you thinking of your "to do" list?

When driving, do you notice the way the shadows of the passing cars glide over the pavement? Perhaps these things seem irrelevant to you. Let us consider something more meaningful. When you are with that special person who is so important to you, do you give them your undivided attention when you listen to them? Or are you formulating your response to them as they are speaking to you? Can you allow others to fully express their sorrow, anger, or fear to you? Or do you try to make them feel better or attempt to persuade them to see your point of view?

Are you aware of thoughts and emotions when they first appear in your awareness? Or do you just find yourself getting angry, worried, frustrated, or depressed because that is the way you feel? Do you experience the moment-to-moment magic of life, or is your attitude toward life that it is "just another day"?

When you take a shower, is your mind elsewhere? Have you ever seen two people so engrossed with the cell phones that they do not share eye contact? Have you ever driven somewhere only to reach your destination without any memory of the trip? Have you ever been distracted while eating something, not realizing that you had completely consumed it? These are just a few examples of a lack of mindfulness.

To live mindfully is to be fully aware of what is happening now, at this moment. When we practice mindfulness, we become aware of everything that is happening within us and around us. Our awareness is concentrated on what we are experiencing at the moment. We experience the moment with complete openness and acceptance.

If we are thinking about what to do, what to say, or how to respond, we cannot be mindful. If we are trying to deny our experience, we are not being mindful. If we are trying to analyze, evaluate, or modify our experience, we cannot be mindful. When we receive all of experience just as it is, with appreciation and gratitude, we are practicing mindfulness.

Mindfulness is not easily understood by most people unless they have personally experienced it. Trying to explain mindfulness is like expressing the joys of eating chocolate mousse to someone who has never eaten it. In our busy, fast-paced society, with all of its distractions, most of us spend a significant portion of our lives not living mindfully. We are unaware of life in the present moment as our minds carry us off to a different time and place. We get caught up in our thoughts of the past or the future, completely oblivious of life's richness.

Mindfulness is not just a spiritual or metaphysical practice engaged in by mystics or seekers. It is a vital aspect of our happiness and a precious gift that comes with being a conscious being. Without mindfulness, we cannot become fully actualized human beings; rather, we become reactive to situations and events. Instead of using our potential to expand our awareness, we live our lives based on a stimulus-response existence.

All of the societal problems, be it violence, intolerance, poverty, hunger, injustice, or the destruction of the environment, are directly linked to our lack of ability to be fully present in our lives. Because we are not fully present, we lack awareness and wisdom when dealing with the challenges we face. As a result, we choose solutions that are based on habit, fear, practicality, or rushed judgment.

To be fully actualized as a human is to access the wisdom and awareness needed to create value, which benefits both ourselves and others. This creation of value can only come from being fully aware of what is happening at the given moment, both within us and outside. Without this awareness, we stumble through life and often create suffering for ourselves and those around us.

Our place in life is intimately connected to all of existence. If you were to pull a single strand of a spider's web, the entire web would experience your pull. Developing mindfulness enables us to respond to life in a manner that considers how our thoughts, feelings, and actions are directly linked to life's web. The quality of our lives is directly proportional to our level of awareness of it.

The Web of Life

Our minds create a sense of separation; however, this is just an illusion. In truth, everything that exists shares the same foundation of existence, which is non-physical in nature. The world of form arises from the formless. Through our eyes, the world may seem to be inhabited by an infinite variety of living and nonliving beings, with each one of them being a separate entity unto itself.

One who has cultivated mindfulness sees unity, not separateness. Without rain, the flower could not exist. Rain comes from clouds. Without clouds, the flower cannot exist. The flower depends on sunlight for photosynthesis, so the flower's existence is dependent on the sun. The soil, which contains nutrients and holds the water for the flower, is also vital for the flower's existence.

The flower is also dependent on the gardener who tends it and looks after its needs, making the gardener also a vital part of the flower's existence. Because the gardener needs to eat, the farm, which supplies the gardener with his food, becomes indirectly vital for the flower's existence.

The raindrop, the cloud, the sun, the soil, the gardener, and the farm are just some of the components that make it possible for the flower to exist. In turn, all of these components owe their existence to living and nonliving beings. At the most essential level of the universe, the true entity of the flower is the entire universe. If just one "component" failed to exist, then the flower could not exist. From this perspective, the flower contains the entire universe while providing evidence for the existence of the universe itself.

Masters of Mindfulness

Do you have a dog or cat? Do you enjoy being around animals? Does being with your pet or around animals have a calming effect on you? There are several reasons why dogs and cats are popular as pets. Your dog does not judge you; your dog has a complete acceptance of who you are. Not only that, your dog fully accommodates whatever is happening at the moment.

Unlike us, animals are not preoccupied with what may happen in the future. Nor do they dwell on the past, not to say that animals cannot anticipate what may happen nor have memories of the past. Memories and anticipation may arise; however, animals are not distracted by these mental activities; they are focused on what is happening in the current moment. We love our pets because they cause us to unconsciously experience our own sense of being present if we allow this to happen. Animals and babies are masters of remaining fully aware of the present moment. Now take a moment to reflect on how you live. How much of your day is spent planning, strategizing, anticipating, or dwelling on your memories?

What Your Focus Says about You

You can always determine what a person values by where they are placing their focus and attention. Most of us will make the noble claim that our spouses, our partners, or our families are the most important things in our lives. Now think for a moment and be honest with yourself. How often do you give these people your complete and undivided attention? By undivided attention, I mean that you are not looking at your electronic device. You are not anticipating what they are about to say. Nor are you formulating a response as they speak to you. You are not thinking about anything else, including yourself.

Most likely, such encounters rarely happen. The sad thing is that this kind of attention is what we all want. We not only want it; we need it. This goes back to why dogs are so popular; they give us their undivided attention.

At the foundation of all of our challenges are thoughts. Inaccurate memories prevent us from finding our keys, and competing thoughts prevent us from giving our loved ones our full attention. However, the problem is not thoughts; it is our relationship that we have with them.

Clearing the Mind's Water

Imagine a clear jar filled with water. At the bottom of the jar lies a layer of sand. The jar is shaken and placed on a table. With the aid of a flashlight, a beam of light is directed at the jar. The beam becomes dispersed as it travels through the murky water, reflected by the grains of sand suspended in it. With time, the sand will settle to the bottom of the jar. This time, when the beam of light passes through the jar, it remains sharp and focused. The jar is a metaphor for our minds. The sand is a metaphor for our thoughts, and the beam of light is a metaphor for our awareness. Collectively, the jar, sand, water, and light become a metaphor for mindfulness. The jar that was shaken is a metaphor for a mind that is not mindful, while the jar with the clear water is a metaphor for a skillful mind, a mind that has been trained in mindfulness.

Emeritus Professor Katherine Weare writes, "Mindfulness involves learning to direct our attention to our experience as it is unfolding, moment by moment, with open-minded curiosity and acceptance. Rather than worrying about what has happened or might happen, mindfulness trains us to respond skillfully to whatever is actually happening right now, be that good or bad. This includes paying close attention to inner states such as thoughts, emotions, and physical sensations, as well as to what is happening in the outside world."

The practice of mindfulness involves learning to focus our attention on that which we are experiencing, at the moment that it is occurring, with a mindset that is open and accepting. To be mindful means to be aware. It means to be aware of the ebb and flow of thoughts, feelings, and sensations within us and the activity and objects around us. It is to be aware of the words and actions that we unleash and their effects on us and others. When we are not mindful, we create suffering for others and ourselves.

When We are not Mindful

Most of humanity is not mindful. Our mind's water is murky with thoughts of the past and the future. We are unaware of the emotions arising within us until it is too late. These undetected emotions infiltrate our minds and become the filter through which we experience the world and ourselves.

Emotions are like tinted sunglasses, but we do not know that we are wearing them. Thoughts also act like tinted sunglasses. Our troubled thoughts and fearful emotions color our experience of life. Conversely, when we experience thoughts of compassion, feelings of caring, and emotions of love, this becomes our experience. By practicing mindfulness, we can train our minds to become aware of the rising and falling of thoughts, feelings, and sensations so that we are not caught off guard by it.

The person who is unskilled in mindfulness does not understand that they are the cause of all their sufferings. Problems occur because we have not learned to see clearly. We are unaware that we are wearing our tinted sunglasses or that our water is murky. Because we do not see clearly, we fail to respond correctly to situations. Additionally, we are unaware of the connection between our action and their ensuing effects. This is guaranteed to keep you from experiencing your psychic powers.

Examples of Mindfulness Practices

Methods for practicing mindfulness are unlimited, as to practice mindfulness simply means being aware of experience. Some of the more common practices include:

- Focusing on your breathing as you inhale and exhale. Through rhythmic breathing, you can learn to control your autonomic nervous system and enhance your mental focus and self-awareness. Even small children can be taught mindful breathing by simply having them place a small stuffed animal on their stomach as they lie on the floor. The child is then instructed to watch the stuffed animal as it rises and falls with the movements of the abdomen during breathing.

- Learning to be aware of those momentary experiences that are normally overlooked, such as hairline cracks in the sidewalk or the individual leaf of a tree.

- Being aware of the transient nature of thoughts and emotions and realizing that they do not define who you are.

- Doing body scans where you use your attention to scan your body from the tip of your toes to the top of your head.

- Taking food, such as a raisin, and exploring it with deep attention, experiencing it with all of your senses.

- Practicing a walking meditation where the person places their focus on the sensations of walking. When performing walking meditations, one places their attention on sensations of their feet touching the ground and leaving it.

- Learning to focus on extending love and compassion toward other people, including strangers. This practice does not involve overt acts; rather, it is experiencing feelings of love and compassion for another. This practice begins with focusing on someone you know and then extending it to strangers, and then ultimately to all beings.

How and Why Mindfulness Works

Imagine that you wade into a river and feel the water rush against you. You move up the river as you feel the water rush by you. You then move further down toward the end of the river; again, you feel the water rush against you. It does not matter where you travel within the river. You feel water rush against you. Additionally, it is the same water that is rushing against you, regardless of where you travel. The river is a metaphor for presence, also known as the present moment or the Now.

No matter what we are doing, when we are doing it, or how we do it, we are experiencing the present moment. The present moment is eternal; there is no beginning or end. The experience of time, past, present, or future is just a construct of the mind; time is illusionary. The perception of time, though illusionary, has profound implications on our experience of life.

Fear is born out of the perception of time. Fear can only exist when anticipating the future. Further, fear is metabolized by the body. When fear and anxiety are ongoing, it breaks down the body. For this reason, people in war zones or other stressful environments seem to age at a faster rate than those not exposed to high levels of stress.

Mindfulness is about quality of life, which is also related to the illusion of time. Our quality of life is sacrificed when we are distracted by fear, anxiety, or the illusions of time. How can we appreciate the profundity of life if we cannot even stay present long enough to enjoy the simple experience of taking a shower?

Slowing Down the Mental Noise

Another benefit of mindfulness is the slowing down of the mental noise in our head, known as thought. Thought is truly a paradox as it is both all-powerful yet powerless. Thoughts are all-powerful because thoughts determine what we focus on, and they are the predecessor to action. Thoughts are powerless because they have no power of their own; all their power is derived from the attention that we give them.

Suppose our thoughts are of what is possible or how to create value for ourselves and others. In that case, this will be our experience of reality. If our thoughts are based on fear, we will make that our reality. When consumed with thought, how can we connect with those we love or make them feel valued? If we are consumed with thoughts, how can we experience the beauty of a sunset, the pleasure of taking a shower, or the appreciation for our own breath? If we are caught up with our thoughts, how can we communicate with the spiritual realm?

Mindfulness and Emotions

A lack of mindfulness is one of the biggest reasons for the unhappiness of humanity. While engaging in thought, we cannot be aware of the emotions and feelings that lie within us. We all have emotions or feelings that we try to avoid experiencing. In fact, the major reason for addictive behaviors, violence, guilt, resentment, and aggression, are due to our efforts to suppress the expression of those emotions and feelings that we find painful. The problem is that emotions and feelings are energy forms. Just as small children, if they feel they are not getting the attention that they desire, they will find ways to express themselves in other ways, such as those just mentioned.

Our emotions are the overriding factor in determining our choices; even rational thinking cannot beat out the power of emotions. Our emotions, especially those that are subconscious, will override rational thinking if we are not aware. Just as with thoughts, emotions within themselves are powerless. They are only as powerful as the amount of attention we give them or when we suppress them. Becoming mindful of your emotions and feelings, as you would with a guest, will allow your emotions to function in a manner that supports you in your wellbeing.

The Movie of Your Life

Imagine that you are in a theater watching a movie. This movie is full of drama, suspense, action, and comedy. You lose awareness of everything that is happening around you as you become totally absorbed by the movie. With each passing scene, you experience a shift in emotion. During the movie, you experience anticipation, concern, fear, anger, happiness, sadness, laughter, and suspense. Your state of being is as though it was on a roller coaster ride as each scene elicits a change in how you feel.

Now imagine this situation. You are watching the same movie. You are enjoying the range of thoughts and emotions that come from experiencing it; however, you are also fully aware of what is happening around you in the theater. You are aware that it is just a movie, and do not get caught up in it. The movie may elicit a wide range of emotions from you; yet a sense of peace or calm remains with you. You enjoy your movie experience fully while never forgetting it is just a movie.

These two scenarios are a metaphor for life. You are the one that is watching the movie, while the movie is your mind. The first scenario represents the lives of most of us. We are totally absorbed in our thoughts, memories, beliefs, and perceptions, all of which contribute to shaping our sense of identity and our experience of life. Without exception, all of our problems and sufferings, individually or collectively, arise because we are absorbed by our minds; we are absorbed by the movie.

Can You Relate?

Rob wakes up Monday morning at 7:00 a.m. and goes for his morning jog. As he is running, he witnesses the beauty and calm of the morning. His sense of well-being is relaxed and calm. Upon returning home, he takes a tumble and sprains his ankle. Now Rob is feeling upset and frustrated; he is in pain.

Due to the accident, he is late for work, making him anxious as he needs to attend an important meeting. He calls work to advise that he will be late. Rob's manager tells him not to worry as the meeting was canceled. Now Rob experiences a sense of relief.

Rob arrives at work when he is informed that his boss wants to speak to him; Rob is now worried. Rob meets with his boss, who tells him that he is receiving a promotion. Rob is now feeling excited and very happy. Rob drives home but winds up in a minor traffic accident; a car rear-ends his new vehicle. Rob is now irate.

This scenario illustrates how Rob's state of being is constantly changing, based on the situations and events that he experiences. Rob went from relaxed, calm, upset, frustrated, anxious, relieved, worried, excited, happy, and irate. There is nothing wrong with experiencing these emotions; our emotions are what make us human. Problems happen when we allow our emotions to determine our state of well-being or our sense of identity.

Rob's state of well-being and identity were being determined by the situations and events he encountered. Most of us are like this; we allow the ever-changing circumstances of our lives to determine how we feel about ourselves and the world around us. We are like the person in the movie theater who is totally absorbed in the movie. We also experience a roller coaster ride of thoughts and emotions; we forget it is just a movie.

There is another way to live, where our state of happiness and well-being are not determined by our situations or circumstances. Nor is it affected by our thoughts and emotions. When in this state of life, our sense of well-being is based solely on the wisdom and understanding of whom we are at deeper levels of our being. To awaken to our psychic powers is to realize that we are connected to the highest planes of the universe. Practicing mindfulness makes this awakening possible.

Time Traveling

We may believe that psychic powers are reserved for the few and take a great amount of time and practice to achieve them. In truth, none of these beliefs are true. You have psychic powers; you just need to develop them. This is because psychic powers are a potentiality that exists within you already. You always had it, and you always will.

The problem is not that you do not have psychic powers; the problem is that you do not realize it. The reason you do not realize it is because you experience illusions of the mind; you are caught up in the movie within your mind. Developing mindfulness is to see through these illusions so that you can claim your psychic powers.

Mindfulness Exercises

The following mindfulness exercises are staggered according to their level of difficulty. Unless you have experience in mindfulness or meditation, it is recommended that you start off with the beginner's exercises and practice them until you feel comfortable with them. Also, you must perform these exercises with an attitude of openness, non-judgment, patience, and persistence. Since the goal of mindfulness is to be aware of the present moment, do not allow your mind to deceive you with any positive or negative thoughts that you may experience while doing these exercises. Allow all thoughts to appear with full acceptance, but keep your focus on the exercises.

Beginner Exercises

Exercise 1: Mindfully Observing

To experience what it is like to perceive the world without self-identification, try this exercise:

1. Sit down and view your surroundings, taking your time to take everything in.
2. When you are ready, close your eyes and allow yourself to relax.
3. Imagine that you are an alien from a distant planet who has arrived on Earth to study it. You have no information about this planet, nor do you have any past experience to draw from. Because of this, you cannot define, identify, analyze, or judge anything that you experience. In other words, you are a blank slate.
4. Now, open your eyes and look at your surroundings again. Take your time.

5. How did your experience of observing compare with your first observation?

If you did not notice any difference between the two observations, practice this exercise until you do. Anytime we incorporate our thoughts while observing, being observed is no longer being viewed purely. Our conceptual thinking is projected onto it. To be able to observe without utilizing conceptual thinking is part of being mindful and present.

In the previous exercise, you hopefully experience, even if only for a brief moment, what it is like to experience life free of conceptual thinking. The mind is conceptual in the way it functions. The mind transforms the information that we receive through our five senses. Whenever we take in information from the environment through perception – touch, sight, hearing, taste, or smell, the mind conceptualizes that information. Mindfulness allows us to transcend the mind to observe its functions and experience life with greater clarity.

Exercise 2: Mindfulness of Thought
For most of us, we spend our lives with a mind that is full of thoughts, and for some people, their minds are so busy that they rarely experience a peaceful mind. Perhaps the simplest and most basic way to learn mindfulness is to learn to focus on the breath. This technique is used in many other forms of meditation. The following exercise will allow you to develop the ability to slow down your thoughts and increase the power of your awareness.

1. Find a place to sit down, making sure that you are comfortable. Try to find a place that offers solitude

and is free of distractions. With practice, you will be able to practice in almost any kind of environment, regardless of the distractions that may exist.

2. Close your eyes and allow yourself to relax. Breathing normally, place your attention on the flow of your breath through your nose. Focus on the sensations that you experience as you inhale and exhale. Notice the sensation of your breath as you inhale. Experience the sensations of air as it enters your nasal cavity and the rising of your chest and abdomen. When exhaling, notice the sensations in your abdomen and chest falling and that of the air leaving your nasal cavity.

3. Continue to observe the flow of breath as it courses through your body. Feel yourself become more and more relaxed with each breath you take.

As you practice this technique, you are bound to experience your mind wandering as you get distracted by thought. As soon as you know that this has happened, gently redirect your focus back to the breath. Do not judge yourself or your experience when losing your concentration, regardless of how often this happens. The more you practice, the more you will be able to maintain your concentration without being distracted.

Similarly, if you experience sensations or emotions that are distracting, do not judge these either. Simply accept these distractions without trying to change or avoid them and continue to focus on your breath. The goal of mindfulness practice is to become aware of thoughts, emotions, and sensations without getting involved. With continued practice, you will discover that these phenomena of the mind and body are not who you are; they are objects of the mind, and you are the one who is aware of them.

Exercise 3: Mindfulness of the Sensations of the Body
Our body experiences innumerable sensations, yet we are so distracted in our daily lives, we often are unaware of them. This mindfulness exercise will help you develop greater awareness of the sensations of your body.

1. Lie down on the floor or a mat. (Using your bed for this exercise is discouraged as you may fall asleep.)
2. Place your attention on the movement of your breath as you inhale and exhale.
3. As you follow your breath, become aware of the sensations of your body. Do you detect a tingling in your feet or hands? Do you sense pressure or stiffness in your back, shoulders, or neck? Allow yourself to experience every sensation that you are aware of. Do not try to change them, ignore them, or judge them as being good or bad. Simply allow yourself to experience them.
4. Notice that the sensations you feel are not stable as they constantly change in their degree of intensity. In contrast, some sensations may seem to appear, disappear, and then reappear.
5. Allow yourself to experience any given sensation for as long as you desire. When you are ready, just move on to another sensation.
6. Be sure to continue breathing as you perform this exercise.
7. Continue to practice this exercise as long as you wish.

Exercise 4: Relaxation

Progressive relaxation is an exercise that relieves stress and promotes relaxation by sequentially tightening the muscles of the body. Besides relaxing the body and developing greater awareness of the body's sensations, doing this exercise before going to bed can be helpful if you have trouble sleeping.

1. Lie down in bed and allow yourself to relax and be comfortable.
2. Focus on your breathing for a few minutes, paying attention to your breath as it travels through your body during inhalation and exhalation.
3. Close your eyes and breathe. Notice how your abdomen rises and falls as your breath flows in and out.
4. Feel the relaxation in your body as you breathe.
5. When you exhale, pay attention to the sensations in your body. Do you feel more relaxed?
6. Curl your toes. Hold them for a few seconds, and then relax. Feel the sensation of relaxation.
7. Tighten your thighs. Hold them for a few seconds, and then relax. Feel the sensation of relaxation. As you breathe out, feel your legs becoming heavier and more relaxed.
8. Tighten the muscles of the buttocks, hold them for a few seconds, and then relax. Feel the sensation of relaxation.
9. Tighten the muscles of your abdomen. Hold them for a few seconds, and then relax. Feel the sensation of relaxation.
10. Take three deep breaths using your diaphragm. As you inhale, focus on your abdomen rising. When

exhaling, focus on your abdomen falling. After taking
three deep breaths, inhale for a fourth breath and
hold it. Hold your breath for as long as you can.
When you exhale, focus on your experience as the air
is released from your body.

11. Raise your shoulders toward your ears, raising them
    as high as possible. Hold them for a few seconds, and
    then relax. Feel the sensation of relaxation in your
    shoulders.
12. Tilt your head back as far as possible. Hold it for a
    few seconds, and then relax. Feel the sensation of
    relaxation in your neck.
13. Raise your head toward your chest. Hold it for a few
    seconds, and then relax. Feel the sensation of
    relaxation in your neck.
14. Tighten your jaw. Hold it for a few seconds, and then
    relax. Feel the sensation of relaxation in your jaw.
15. Raise your brow as high as possible. Hold it for a few
    seconds, and then relax. Feel the sensation of
    relaxation in your face.
16. Tighten your brow as much as possible. Hold it for a
    few seconds, and then relax. Feel the sensation of
    relaxation in your face.
17. Take time just to relax and enjoy the sensations of
    your body.

Exercise 5: Mindful Walking

Mindfulness can be practiced anywhere and at any time. A
great way to do this is through mindful walking.

When first practicing this exercise, it helps to start off with
designating a short distance (approximately ten feet). You will

practice mindful walking. As you get more comfortable with this exercise, you can extend the distance.

With your route marked out, walk at a relaxed pace the distance of your route. As you walk, place your awareness on the sensation that you experience as your feet make contact with the ground and when they leave it. Make sure as you are walking that you continue to breathe.

As you become more skillful in focusing on the sensations of walking, you can extend your awareness to what is happing in your environment. Listen to the sound of birds singing, the wind blowing, the sound of cars, or the sound of people talking. As always, in mindfulness practice, do not judge, analyze, or evaluate anything that you experience; your only job is to be aware.

Exercise 6: Mindfulness in Eating
Have you ever eaten while watching television or talking to someone, then come to the realization that you have consumed your meal without any memory of doing so? Perhaps, you realized that you ate your meal but had no memory of really tasting it? When we eat this way, we are not mindful of our eating. As a matter of fact, many problems with digestion or maintaining our proper weight are due, in part, to not eating mindfully. When we are not eating mindfully, we deny ourselves savoring our food as our minds are elsewhere.

When practicing mindful eating, it is important to set up your environment to not be distracted as you eat. You can eat alone or find someone who would be interested in eating mindfully with you, which means that there is to be no conversation while eating. Also, turn off all electronic devices and make sure you have everything you need to enjoy your meal to avoid getting up to get something while eating. Lastly, it is recommended that you eat a healthy meal. As the purpose of practicing mindfulness is mental wellbeing, you also want to enjoy physical health as well. Here is an exercise for mindful eating.

1. Take time to relax and focus on your breath. Allow yourself to relax.
2. When you are ready, take a look at your food, and observe its color, shape, and texture.
3. Take in its aroma. How does your food smell? Is its aroma weak, mild, or strong?
4. Now taste your food, but do so mindfully. Take only bite-size pieces and take your time before swallowing them. Allow yourself to savor its taste and how it feels in your mouth.
5. When you are ready, swallow your food.

Exercise 7: Showering Mindfully

How many times have you taken a shower, only to realize while your body was in the shower, your mind was elsewhere? You can practice mindfulness in everything you do, and showering is no different. Taking a shower mindfully is a great way to become more in touch with your body, sensations, and awareness of the present moment.

When taking a shower, you want your full attention on the experience of taking a shower, not on your memories of the past or your thoughts of the future. Your only job is to take in all the sensory experiences of taking a shower. It is only natural that while taking a shower that thought will arise, which is okay. Do not react to your thoughts; just ignore them and return your attention to the sensations of taking a shower. Allow yourself to experience whatever is happening at that moment. As you take your shower, place your focus on what you are experiencing. Here are some examples:

- Place your attention on the feelings of the water running down your body.
- Feel the sensation of the water against your skin.
- Listen to the sound of your breath.
- Listen to the sound of the water cascading downward.
- Smell the shampoo or soap that you are using.
- Feel the sensations of the soles of your feet on the shower floor.
- Feel the sensations as you work the shampoo into your hair.
- Watch as the water glides down your body.
- Watch the water as it flows down the shower drain.
- Watch the water drops splatter as they make contact with the shower floor.

Exercise 8: Mindful Observing
Find a place that is comfortable for you. It can be indoors or outdoors. Sit down and allow yourself to relax. For the next 10 minutes, simply observe everything around you. Observe what you experience from within yourself (i.e., thoughts, emotions, sensations, or feelings). Whatever it is that you

notice, do not judge, evaluate, or analyze it. You are just to observe it. Feel free to go longer if you can.

Practice this each day, increasing the observation time each day. When doing this exercise, you should stay relaxed. You cannot get this exercise wrong. Even if you catch yourself making a judgment, allow yourself to experience this without judgment.

Exercise 9: Mindful Waking

Practicing mindfulness can happen the moment you open your eyes when you wake up. Rather than ignoring your alarm clock or bolting out of bed, take time to place your awareness on the sensations of your body. Take note of how you are feeling. Be aware of your thoughts. Spend time just taking stock of what you are experiencing. Before getting out of bed, take the time to stretch your limbs and back while noting the sensations.

Exercise 10: Mindful Cleaning

When doing chores, place your complete focus on the task that you are doing. Housework is an excellent opportunity to practice mindfulness, whether doing the dishes, the laundry, sweeping, dusting, cleaning, or vacuuming. Regardless of the task that is being performed, observe the following guidelines:

- Place your full attention on the task that you are doing. If you are doing the dishes, place your focus on everything that you experience while doing the dishes. Here are a few examples:
- Focus on the sensation of the water.
- Focus on the sensation of cleaning the dish.

- Focus on the sensations of your body's movements while doing the dishes.
- Focus on the movement of the water and soap suds.
- Focus on the dirt being removed.
- Be aware of the sounds in your environment.
- Focus on any smells that you detect.

When doing the task, do not judge anything that happens. Do not think about completing the task or what you will be doing when you finish the dishes. Focus only on the process of washing dishes. When doing the task, perform it from the spirit of gratitude or appreciation.

Example: Be grateful for the fact that you have dishes or water to clean them. Be appreciative that you have food to put on the dishes. Be appreciative that cleaning dishes is an act of love to those who will be eating off them. When performing the task, slow down from your normal pace to more fully experience what is happening.

Exercise 11: Mindful Waiting

Whenever you find yourself waiting in line or caught in a traffic jam, you can practice mindfulness by focusing on all that there is to experience. Start off by placing your attention on your breath. Be aware of your breathing, the sensations in your body, and then let your attention drift as you take in your environment. The following are examples of what you could be aware of:

- The arising and passing of thought.

- The arising and passing of emotions or feelings.
- The arising and passing of sensations.
- The people around you.
- The objects in your environment.
- The colors and textures in your environment.
- The sounds in your environment.
- The smells in your environment.
- The level of happiness of the people around you.
- Things that you can be grateful or appreciative for.

Exercise 12: Allowing of the Body
The following exercise is good for learning to be mindful of your body. To do this exercise, do the following:
1. Sit in a chair or on a pillow and allow yourself to be comfortable.
2. Close your eyes and relax.
3. Allow your awareness to roam freely; do not try to focus on anything particular.
4. Now place your awareness on the body. Allow your body to move any way it wants. Do not try in any way to control your posture or the way you are sitting. Whatever your body is telling you, allow your body to assume that movement or positioning.
5. Enjoy the allowing of your body. Maintain this allowing for as long as you desire.

Intermediate Exercises
Exercise 1: Mindfulness of sensation
1. Close your eyes and allow yourself to relax.
2. Follow your breath during inhalation and exhalation.

Allow your awareness to wash over your body and experience its sensations.

3. When you come across a pleasant sensation, place your focus on it.

4. As you focus on the pleasant sensation, ask yourself, "What is the color of this sensation?" Trust whatever answer comes to you, going by the first answer that you receive. If you are unable to name the color, that is okay. What is more important is that you recognize it as having a color.

5. Next, ask yourself: "What size is this sensation?" Is it tiny or big? Again, go by your first impressions.

6. Next, ask yourself if the sensation has a texture to it. Does the sensation seem hard, soft, light, or heavy?

7. Remember the qualities of the pleasant sensation (You may want to write them down).

8. Next, find a sensation that feels unpleasant. Repeat steps 5-8 with this sensation.

9. When you have all your information, compare the qualities of the pleasant sensation with the unpleasant one. Is there a difference?

10. This next step is optional and requires a good imagination to do. Using the qualities of the pleasant sensation, imagine that you are pouring them on the unpleasant sensation. If the color of the pleasant sensation was orange and the unpleasant sensation was black, imagine the black turning to orange. Repeat this process with the remaining two qualities.

11. When you have done this, do you experience a change in the way the unpleasant sensation feels?

Exercise 2: Exercises for Mindfulness of Emotions

We often let our thoughts and emotions get the upper hand in our lives and influence our decisions. In this exercise, you will learn to master your emotions instead of letting them master you. Inherently, our thoughts and emotions are powerless; we personalize them that they gain power.

1. Find a quiet place where you will not be disturbed and make yourself comfortable.

2. When relaxed, close your eyes and place your attention on your breath. For approximately one minute, follow the path of your breath as it travels through your body. Do this by focusing on the sensations that you experience. If you wish to extend this step for more than one minute, allow yourself to do so.

3. Adopt the attitude that you will allow anything that you experience to appear before you. Do not resist or try to change anything. Let everything that appears to do so without judging it.

4. If you experience an unpleasant thought or emotion, allow yourself to observe it as a birdwatcher observes a rare bird from a distance. Simply observe it calmly without getting involved with it.

5. As you observe the thought or emotion, what happens to it? Does it get weaker, fainter? The change in potency happens because you are no longer giving it power. That thought or emotion depended on you for its power.

Exercise 3: Mindfulness of Observing
This exercise is very similar to the first exercise in the beginning section, but it takes it one step further.

1. Find a place that is comfortable for you. It can be indoors or outdoors.
2. Sit down and allow yourself to relax. For the next 10 minutes, simply observe everything around you. Observe what you experience from within yourself (i.e., thoughts, emotions, sensations, or feelings).
3. When observing, do not judge anything that you experience. Do not get involved in any thinking while observing. Observe with an awareness that is pure and untouched by thinking. When thoughts arise, acknowledge their existence and return your attention to observing.
4. If you can go with this exercise longer than 10 minutes, allow yourself to do so if you desire.

Practice this each day, increasing the observation time each day. When doing this exercise, you should stay relaxed. You cannot get this exercise wrong. Even if you catch yourself making a judgment, allow yourself to experience this without judgment.

Chapter 9: Meditation

The purpose of meditation is to redirect our attention from the outer world and place it in our inner world. Our outer world is a projection of our inner world; only when you understand your inner world can you move beyond the illusions of the mind. When meditating, we are shining the light of awareness on the mental phenomena that create our experience of reality, which brings about a harmonious mind.

When you can get clarity of your inner world, you will use your psychic energy with greater precision. Meditation is about becoming aware of the present moment. It means that everything that we experience while meditating is valid. When performing these exercises, allow all thoughts to appear, but do not hold onto any of them.

Guidelines for Practicing Meditation

Before we launch into the first meditation, I want to share some helpful guidelines that will make your meditation experience more enjoyable. The first guideline is to throw out all the rules! I am talking about the rules or expectations you have for yourself, your expectations for what you want to experience, and your beliefs of what should or should not happen.

Whatever enters your awareness during the exercises, allow it to happen. Do not try to resist, change, control, or modify anything that is experienced— the best meditative experiences are when we give up all effort to make things happen.

Your only job is to witness what you are experiencing as you dive down into the deeper realms of consciousness. The practice of meditation is not about becoming something different. Instead, it is about remembering the truth of who you are.

The following mindfulness exercises are staggered according to their level of difficulty. It is important to be comfortable with each exercise before progressing to the next one. When performing these exercises, approach them with openness, non-judgment, patience, and persistence.

The goal of meditation is to become aware of the present moment. Do not hold on to any positive or negative thoughts that you may have while meditating. Allow all thoughts to appear with full acceptance, but keep your focus on the exercises.

Meditation 1: Contemplating Awareness

The purpose of this exercise is to challenge your sense of relationship with your environment. We were raised believing that who we are is a separate entity from that which we are experiencing. In other words, when I look at my dog, I see him as being a separate being or object that exists outside me. Note: You will be asking yourself a number of questions when performing this exercise. Answer the questions based solely on your direct experience at that moment, not what you know intellectually.

1. Sit down and allow yourself to relax.
2. Breathing naturally, place your attention on the flow of your breath as you inhale and exhale, noticing the sensations that you experience.
3. When you feel relaxed, select an object for observing.
4. Observe the object for a few seconds, allowing your eyes to be relaxed. Do not strain them.
5. As you observe the object, determine whether the act of seeing is separate from the object or not. In other words, does seeing stop at a certain point, at which the object begins, or does the act of seeing and the object being seen merge into each other as one?
6. Now, determine if the act of seeing begins from within you or if it occurs from the outside of the body.
7. Next, ask yourself if you are aware of seeing. In other words, how do you know that the act of seeing is taking place? Note: The question is regarding the process of seeing, not that which is being seen. How do you know the process of seeing is occurring? Are you aware that "seeing" is taking place? As indicated before, do not think of the correct answer to this question; only go by your direct experience at this moment.

8. Confirm to yourself that seeing and the object being seen are not separate, that they indeed flow into each other as one.

9. Confirm to yourself that seeing occurs from within the body, not outside of it.

10. Confirm to yourself that there is the awareness of seeing that there is a knowing that seeing is taking place at some level of your being.

If you can confirm all of these points, we are left with the following conclusions:

- The process of seeing and the object being seen are inseparable; they are one.

- Seeing originates from within you. From this, we can logically conclude that both the process of seeing and the object being seen are found within you.

- There must be awareness of seeing taking place; otherwise, how would you know that seeing occurs?

- The process of seeing and the object that is being seen occur within awareness.

- You are aware of your existence.

- You, the process of seeing, and the object being seen are inseparable; they are all the same.

- You, the process of seeing and the object being seen are found in awareness.

- You are awareness itself.

Suppose you can directly experience these conclusions for yourself. In that case, you will be light years ahead of most of humanity, which believes that they are a separate object. All problems arise from seeing ourselves as being separate. As long as we see ourselves as being separate from those around us, we will always experience limitation, lack, and frustration. We will also struggle to experience our psychic powers. The previous exercise can be repeated with the remaining sensory modalities as well. The following exercise uses the sense of touch.

Sensation or Touch

1. Close your eyes and touch an object.
2. Confirm to yourself that the sensations of the object being touched and the object itself are not separate, that they indeed flow into each other as one.
3. Confirm to yourself that sensation arises from within the body, not outside of it.
4. Confirm to yourself that there is the awareness that the act of touching is taking place.
5. Confirm for yourself that the awareness of touching and the act of touching are inseparable.
6. Confirm that there is an awareness of your own existence.

If you can confirm all of these points, we are left with the following conclusions:

- When touching (with closed eyes), we cannot distinguish between the sensation of the object and the object being touched.
- Sensation originates from within you. From this, we can logically conclude that both the process of

touching and the object being touched is found within you.

- There must be awareness that touching is taking place; otherwise, how would we know that act of touching was occurring?
- The awareness of touching and the act of touching are inseparable.
- The sensation of the object and the object being touched occurs within awareness.
- You are aware of your existence.
- You, the act of touching, the sensation of the object, and the object being touched are inseparable; they are one and the same.
- You are awareness itself.

Meditation 2: Perceiving Thought

In this meditation, you will increase your awareness of thought.

1. Sit down in a comfortable position and close your eyes.
2. Follow your breath during inhalation and exhalation. Place your attention on your breath. Feel it as it courses through your body.
3. Take on an attitude of complete allowing that you will have complete acceptance of whatever arises in this meditation.
4. Observe the perceptions, thoughts, sensations, and emotions that arise within you. Allow them to come and go on their own accord. All you need to do is to be the observer of them.
5. Now place your attention on your thoughts. Observe your thoughts as they appear and fade in the space of

your awareness. Remain as the observer. Do not judge, evaluate, or analyze your thoughts; allow them to be just as they are. Simply be aware of them.

6. You may find yourself experience racing thoughts. Just acknowledge that your thoughts are racing.

7. Do not judge your experience should you experience disturbing thoughts. Your thoughts have no power other than that which you give them. Let your thoughts move freely in and out of your awareness. Stay as the observer; nothing else is needed.

8. Now follow a thought from the time it arises to the time it fades away. Through your observing, can you find the place where thoughts arise from? This question is not to be thought about; its answer needs to be observed and experienced by you.

9. Where do thoughts go when they disappear from awareness? Can you observe this?

10. Notice that after a thought fades, there is a space or emptiness before the next thought appears. Place your attention on this space. Should you become distracted, simply return your attention to this space between your thoughts. Do not exert any effort in this observation; do not try to locate this space; simply allow yourself to be the observer.

11. Can you know a thought before it appears in your awareness?

12. If you can observe your thoughts, can you be your thoughts?

13. This is the end of this meditation. Feel free to remain silent and still for as long as your desire.

Meditation 3: Cultivating Super Emotions

Super emotions include gratitude, appreciation, and compassion. They are called super emotions because of their high vibrational frequency. The following meditations are for cultivating these emotions.

Gratitude

1. Sit down in a chair or on a pillow, whichever is most comfortable for you.
2. Close your eyes and place your attention on your breath as you breathe normally.
3. Place your awareness on the sensations that you experience as your breath enters your body during inhalation and leaves it during exhalation.
4. Allow yourself to experience everything that arises in your awareness without any form of judgment or resistance. Greet every experience with complete acceptance.
5. Anytime you find yourself becoming distracted, gently return your awareness to your breath.
6. Everything that you experience is an opportunity to express gratitude:
     - You can experience gratitude for a person, a pet, or for nature.
     - You can express gratitude for the challenges you have experienced and what you gained from them.
     - You can express gratitude for being alive.
7. Think of someone or something that you can be grateful for.

8. When you have selected the object of your gratitude, ask yourself why you are grateful for them. Think of all the reasons why you are grateful.

    As you think about this, pay attention to the feelings that you are experiencing.

9. When you find yourself experiencing gratitude, try to intensify that feeling. Place your awareness on the feeling of gratitude. What happens when you focus on the emotion of gratitude? You can use this technique to intensify any emotion or feeling that you experience.

10. Allow yourself to experience the emotion of gratitude as deeply as possible.

11. If you have trouble with this exercise, keep practicing it until you experience the level of gratitude that you desire.

Appreciation

1. Sit down in a comfortable position and close your eyes.

2. Now breathe deeply, hold your breath briefly, and then exhale.

3. Feel the relaxation in your body.

4. Feel yourself becoming more and more relaxed.

5. Follow your breath during inhalation and exhalation. Place your attention on your breath. Feel it as it courses through your body.

6. Think of someone or something that you love. As you think of your subject, think of all the ways that you appreciate them.

7. Fully experience your feelings.

8. As you experience these energies, intensify them by employing your other senses, such as touch, hearing,

smelling, and taste. To do this, add these other sensory dimensions to your mind's representation of your subject. Example: If I am thinking of my spouse, I would also imagine her touching me, hearing her voice, smell her perfume, and tasting her kiss.

9. By engaging your other senses, the feelings of appreciation will be experienced more deeply.

10. We are now going to switch gears. For this exercise, think of a person that you have neutral feelings for. For example, it could be the store clerk where you do your shopping or the person who delivers your mail.

11. Think about what you can appreciate about this person.

12. As before, fully experience the feelings that you are having and try to intensify them.

13. Now think of someone who irritates you.

14. Think about what you can appreciate about them.

15. Fully experience the feelings that you are having and try to intensify them.

16. Now think of someone who you hate.

17. What can you appreciate about them?

18. Fully experience the feelings that you are having and try to intensify them.

19. Now think about yourself. What can you appreciate about yourself?

20. Fully experience the feelings that you are having and try to intensify them.

21. The level of your appreciation has less to do with the world around you than it does with your ability to take charge of your energy level. Emotional mastery is the ability to generate appreciation for any experience that you may have.

22. This is the end of this exercise.

Compassion

The following is an exercise for expanding your compassion. This exercise is really a series of sub-exercises, with each one creating the foundation for the following exercise.

Step 1:

I want you to think of a person or animal that you love.

Think about the hardships and challenges that they have experienced. Think of the sufferings that they have experienced and make their suffering your own. When you have connected with their sufferings, express your love to them, and wish them happiness.

Step 2:

In this next exercise, you will repeat what you did in the first exercise; however, this time, you will choose a subject that you have neutral feelings for. For example, your subject could be the clerk at the register where you do your shopping or the mailperson.

Even though you may not know anything about this person, I want you to imagine the sufferings that they may have experienced in their life. Use your intuition or your imagination but make their suffering as real as you can. Allow yourself to experience their sufferings as your own. When you have connected with their sufferings, wish them happiness.

Step 3:

In this third exercise, you will repeat what you did in the last two exercises using another subject. In this exercise, your subject will be someone you dislike, avoid, or do not get along with. I want you to think of the sufferings that they have experienced in their life. As in the previous exercise, you can use your intuition or imagination if you do not know this person's background. Allow yourself to experience their sufferings as your own. When you have connected with their sufferings, wish them happiness.

Step 4:

This exercise differs from the previous three exercises because you will not be identifying your subject ahead of time. Instead, you perform this compassion exercise as you go about your day. I want you to notice the people around you as you conduct your daily business. Take time to imagine the potential sufferings of the people that you see. Allow yourself to experience their sufferings as your own. When you have connected with their sufferings, wish them happiness.

Step 5:

This is the final exercise, and for many people, the most difficult one. In this exercise, you will be the subject of your meditation. I want you to reflect on the sufferings that you have experienced in your life. Allow yourself to experience your sufferings fully; do not minimize anything. Get in touch with the pains that you have experienced. When you have connected with your sufferings, wish happiness for yourself.

The exercise that you just completed was an exercise in experiencing compassion. The subject of your compassion began with the ones that are the easiest for us to experience compassion for, those we love. Each succeeding exercise became more difficult because the subject of your compassion became further removed from you emotionally.

Most people have trouble showing compassion for themselves, which is why you were the subject in the final meditation. The power of your compassion for others is dependent on your ability to have compassion for yourself.

When we lack compassion for others, we lack compassion for ourselves; we project our lack of compassion for ourselves on those around us. Conversely, when you develop compassion for yourself, you can truly have compassion for others. The power of compassion is also vital if you are to increase your vibration to a higher level.

Meditation 4: Spiritual Love

To experience your psychic powers, you need to raise your vibrational level. Our relationships are one of the most influential areas of our lives when impacting our vibratory levels. For this exercise, you will be introduced to spiritual relationships.

In traditional relationships, each partner looks to the other partner to fulfill their needs. There is an unwritten expectation that our partner needs to make us happy. Since no person can fulfill all the needs of another, disappointments are inevitable. When this happens, we may feel insecure and feel that our partner does not love us any more or may leave us. This often leads to control issues and resentment. In a spiritual relationship, each partner supports the other in becoming the best that they can be.

For a spiritual relationship to work, both partners need to have the same desire to transcend the conventions of an ordinary relationship and be committed to self-discovery. For this reason, this meditation is intended only for you, the listener. Do not try to get your partner to accept what you have learned from this exercise. Instead, use what you learned to improve the quality of your relationship by becoming a better partner.

   1.   Sit down in a comfortable position and close your eyes.

2.   Now breathe deeply, hold your breath briefly, and then exhale.

3.   Feel the relaxation in your body.

4.   Follow your breath during inhalation and exhalation. Place your attention on your breath. Feel it as it courses through your body.

5.   Sink deeper and deeper into relaxation.

6.   You are about to be asked to remember some situations in your past relationships. While there are some memories you may want to avoid thinking about, know that you are safe as long as you are willing to revisit that memory and that you do not judge it. Remember, you are not your thoughts, and your memories are a form of thought. Who you are is the one that is aware of thought.

7.   We often seek relationships out of the belief that finding the right person will make us happy. We may believe that all of our current problems will be alleviated if we were with that special someone.

8.   When we enter a relationship with someone, we are full of hope and excitement. Suddenly the world is a better place. As long as that person meets our expectations, we feel happy. We feel that our lives have taken a turn for the better.

9.   However, if our partner behaves in a way that goes against our expectations, we become concerned, insecure, or fearful.

10. Breathe deeply, hold your breath briefly, and then exhale.

11. Feel the relaxation in your body.

12. Feel yourself becoming more and more relaxed.

13. Follow your breath during inhalation and exhalation. Place your attention on your breath.

14. Now think of a specific time in the past when your partner did something that went against your expectations. Try to relive this situation in as much detail as you can. Replay this situation in your mind as though it was a movie.

15. As you replay this memory, what do you see?

16. What do you hear? Are you and your partner talking? What are you saying?

17. As you sense that your relationship has taken a wrong turn, what are you feeling?

18. Are you concerned?

19. Are you in denial of how you feel?

20. Do you feel numb?

21. Are you fearful?

22. If you feel any of these feelings, you based your sense of happiness on the expectations that your partner would meet your needs. As soon as your expectations were not met, your sense of happiness became threatened.

23. Often, our sense of who we are is shaped by our relationships.

24. When our sense of happiness or identity is based on something outside of ourselves, our happiness will be unstable. True happiness can only exist when our source of happiness is non-changing.

25. Now go back to your memory of the situation with your partner. How did you react to your partner when they did not meet your expectations?

26. What was their response to your reaction?

27. Most likely, your partner felt defensive as you were threatening their sense of freedom to be who they are.

28. Whenever we have expectations of others to make us feel good about ourselves, we are hurting both ourselves and our relationship with the other person. We suffer because we are looking in the wrong place for lasting happiness, and our partner is being pressured to be something other than who they are.

29. Now go back to your memory of the situation.

30. Get in touch with what you were feeling at the time.

31. At the time, your reaction to your partner was triggered by the emotions that you were experiencing.

32. For a brief amount of time, you became your emotions.

33. Previously in this book, you learned to observe emotions.

34. Now breathe deeply, hold your breath briefly, and then exhale.

35. Feel the relaxation in your body.

36. Feel yourself becoming more and more relaxed.

37. Follow your breath during inhalation and exhalation. Place your attention on your breath. Feel it as it courses through your body.

38. Once again, go back to the emotion that you were feeling at the time.

39. Place your attention on it. Make it the object of your attention. Do so with complete acceptance. Do not try to change it or resist it.

40. What happens to this emotion when you observe it with complete acceptance?

41. You did not need anyone or anything to change how you felt. If you were successful with this portion of the

meditation, you could change how you felt without any effort.

42. Being able to observe your emotions as they appear in your awareness is very powerful. You develop self-mastery. To be able to do this is to be practicing mindfulness.

43. Now go back to your memory of the situation.

44. See yourself reacting toward your partner.

45. As soon as you notice the emotion arising, shift your attention away from your partner and toward the emotion. Observe it with complete acceptance.

46. When your emotion loses its potency, ask yourself this question: "What can I say or do that will benefit both my partner and me?"

47. When you ask this question, you transform conflict into an opportunity for personal growth for both of you.

    You will be able to share your concerns with your partner in a way that respects each other's dignity.

48. Now breathe deeply, hold your breath briefly, and then exhale.

49. Feel the relaxation in your body.

50. Feel yourself becoming more and more relaxed.

51. Follow your breath during inhalation and exhalation. Place your attention on your breath.

52. Now go back to the memory of the situation.

53. See yourself observing your emotions instead of reacting to your partner.

54. As your emotion loses its potency, ask yourself, "What can I do to support my partner so that he or she can get what they want?"

55. Next, ask yourself, "What do I need to do to take care of myself?"

56. See yourself doing what you need to do to support both yourself and your partner in becoming happy.

57. You are in the beginning stages of experiencing spiritual love. In spiritual love, we free our partners from our expectations and allow them to be their authentic selves. When we free our partner, we free ourselves.

58. Because we are free, we can support our partners as they travel their own path. To do this is the greatest gift that we can give another person.

59. True love is the ability to give our partners the freedom to be themselves, even at the risk of losing them.

60. Spiritual relationships start and end with us.

61. It comes from establishing a secure sense of self.

62. A secure sense of self comes from realizing that the essence of who we are is love itself.
    Now breathe deeply, hold your breath briefly, and then exhale.

63. Feel the relaxation in your body.

64. Now say to yourself: "Everything that I encounter in life is there to support me in my growth." How does that feel when you say this?

65. Say it again with even more conviction: "Everything that I encounter in life is there to support me in my growth." Experience what you feel when you say this. Say it now.

66. One last time, say it with meaning: "Everything that I encounter in life is there to support me in my growth." Experience what you feel when you say this. Say it now.

67. Now breathe deeply, hold your breath briefly, and then exhale.

68. Relax.

69. Now breathe normally. As you breathe, place your attention on your breath. Notice the sensations that you experience as your breath travels into your body during inhalation and when it leaves your body during exhalation.

70. Feel yourself becoming more and more relaxed. Enjoy the feeling.

71. Continue to follow your breath as it enters and leaves your body.

72. Accept everything that enters your awareness without any judgment.

73. Feel yourself going deeper and deeper within. Allow yourself to surrender to everything that you experience.

74. Continue to breathe and remain aware of the flow of your breath.

75. Now make the intention: "Everything that I encounter in life is there to support me in my growth. "Do not hold on to this intention. As soon as you are aware of it, let it go. Release your intention to the universe.

76. By practicing letting go, you allow the universe to organize the situations and events that will support you in making your intention a reality.

77. This is the end of this meditation. When you awake, know that you will be guided by life toward achieving your intention each day. Treat each experience as a teacher who is there to point the way.

Meditation 5: Self-Love

The previous exercises provided guidance for cultivating super emotions. This meditation for cultivating self-love will draw from these exercises.

1. While looking into a mirror, look deeply into your eyes and tell yourself out loud, "I love you," using your name.
2. Attempt to feel love for yourself. If you can experience feelings of love, allow yourself to experience them as fully as possible. If you are unable to experience loving feelings, do not force it. Simply remain aware of any feelings that should arise without judgment.
3. Continue to look into your eyes while telling yourself, "I love you," using your name.
4. As you address yourself in this manner, place your focus on any emotions of appreciation, compassion, or gratitude that you may experience.
5. You can tap into these emotions if you recall things you have done that you feel good about. Incorporate all these memories in the way that you address yourself, for example: "I love you (include your name) for the way you did..."
6. Focus on the feelings of love or appreciation that you experience as you do this exercise. As you do so, try to intensify these feelings.
7. Try to do this exercise every morning and evening, allowing five minutes per exercise. Do this exercise daily until you begin to experience feelings of love for yourself.

Meditation 6: The Body's Energy and Decision Making

In this exercise, you will use your awareness of the body's sensations to make decisions based on the profound wisdom of life's energy. This exercise will also help you become more sensitive to the sensations that accompany your intuitive moment.

1. Sit down in a comfortable position and close your eyes.
2. Follow your breath during inhalation and exhalation. Place your attention on your breath. Feel it as it courses through your body. Allow yourself to relax.
3. I want you now to think of a decision that you need to make. If you currently do not have a decision to make, create one that is relevant to you.
4. Next, think of all the choices that are available to you when making your decision.
5. Now think of the potential costs and benefits for each choice option. For example, if I had to decide whether to buy a new car, I would consider the costs and benefits of each choice. Example: If I decide to buy the car, I would have a new car, but I would use all my savings.

    When doing this part of the meditation, do not over-analyze the situation; just go by whatever answer comes to you. This is not intended to be an intellectual meditation.
6. Now return your attention to your breath and allow yourself to relax. Do not engage with any of your thoughts; allow yourself to become relaxed and still within.

7. Now, while remaining in your peacefulness, review your potential choices, one by one. Consider each choice separately, giving each your full attention.

8. As you review the choice, ask yourself, "Should I say yes to this choice option?" When you do this, pay attention to the sensations that you experience in your body.

9. When you think of this choice option, do you feel constricted or relaxed? Is your breathing relaxed or shallow? Does your chest feel hard or soft? Does your body feel dense or tingly? Notice the sensations of the body and the quality of your breathing as you reflect on each option.

10. Without exception, you were intended to be happy in this life. Happiness is your birthright. Which option brings you the greatest sense of peacefulness in your body? Which option brings about the greatest ease in your breathing? Regardless of what your mind or conventional wisdom says, that is the option that is right for you.

11. As before, if you had difficulty experiencing the body's sensations as you considered your choices, please practice this meditation until you can do so. Do not continue to the next meditation until you do.

12. This is the end of this meditation.

Meditation 7: Letting Go and Allowing

It is my hope that by now that you realize that nothing in your experience is permanent. Your thoughts, perceptions, and sensation are constantly appearing and disappearing. Further, there is nothing in your experience that does not arise from within you. Did you know of the thought, perceptions, and sensations before they revealed themselves to you? No, you did not. These phenomena simply arise and fade within the space of your awareness on their own accord. So what are you holding on to? What are you trying to control? This next meditation is about allowing.

1. Sit down and make yourself comfortable; allow yourself to relax. If you would like, you may close your eyes for now.

2. Allow yourself to relax as you focus on your breath, place your attention on your breath as it enters your body, travels through your body, and then leaves it as you exhale.

3. Breathe normally, without exerting any effort. Relax.

4. Allow yourself to develop a sense of total acceptance. Be totally allowing of what appears in your awareness.

5. Do not judge, evaluate, or analyze anything that you experience.

6. Do not hold any expectations for what you should be experiencing.

7. Do not search for anything. Do not imagine or create anything. Simply observe.

8. If unpleasant or uncomfortable thoughts, feelings, or sensations arise, let them be.

9. Allow them to come into your awareness. Do not try to change them. Do not try to replace them with something more pleasant or positive.

10. If you feel numbness, or a sense of dullness, allow this too.

11. You cannot do anything wrong. Whatever you are experiencing, this is the right experience for you.

12. Allow your experience to flow through your awareness. All that is needed from you is to be aware of them.

13. There is nothing for you to do. There is nothing for you to change. There is nothing for you to believe. Simply be the observer of all that presents itself.

14. This is the end of this meditation. Allow yourself to remain in silence for as long as you desire.

Meditation 8: Self-Inquiry

In this book, you experienced a number of meditations, many of which posed questions for you to ask yourself. Anytime we ask our self a question, we are engaging in self-inquiry. You will now engage in self-inquiry on the biggest question you can ever ask yourself: Who are you?

1. Sit down in a comfortable position and close your eyes.

2. Allow yourself to follow your breath during inhalation and exhalation. Place your attention on your breath. Feel it as it courses through your body.

3. Take on an attitude of total acceptance for whatever arises in this meditation.

4. Observe the perceptions, thoughts, and sensations that arise within you. Allow them to come and go on their own accord. All you need to do is be the observer of them. To observe them is to be aware of them.

5. You are the observer of thoughts, perceptions, and sensations. You are the one that is aware of experience. But who are you? You refer to yourself as "I," who is this "I"?

6. Where is this "I" located? Is it located in your body? Is it located in your heart?

7. The word "phenomenal" means something that can be seen, thought, touched, heard, or detected somehow.

8. When you ask yourself, "Where am I located?" any response you come up with will be a phenomenal response.

9. Anything you experience is phenomenal; everything you know is phenomenal.

10. You may experience space, emptiness, or bliss, but even these things are not who you are. Space, emptiness, and bliss can also be detected by you.

11. Are you phenomenal? Everything that is phenomenal changes. Your thoughts, sensations, and perceptions are constantly changing.

12. Your thoughts come in and out of awareness. Who is observing thoughts coming in and out of awareness? Are you coming in and out of awareness?

13. Your sensations are constantly changing. Are you constantly changing?

14. The essence of who you are does not change; it is eternal.

15. No matter what your responses are to these questions, there is awareness of your response. What is aware of your responses?

16. When answering these questions, do not rely on your thinking. You will not get the correct answer.

17. Do not use your imagination or your mind. Neither of these will answer these questions.

18. Do not put in any effort in answering these questions. Just observe. Just be allowing.

19. Who you are cannot be observed; it cannot be felt, and it cannot be detected. Who you are is not phenomenal.

20. Who you are cannot be experienced. Who you are is awareness itself. Just as a ray of light cannot shine on itself, the awareness that is you cannot observe itself. Yet you have a knowing that you exist.

21. Though you cannot perceive yourself, you can perceive that which you are not. You are not your experiences.

22. You are not your experience of life, nor are you your experience of yourself.

23. The more you discover that which you are not, the closer you will come to realize who you are.

24. This is the end of this meditation. Allow yourself to remain in silence for as long as you desire.

Incorporating Mindfulness and Meditation Into Your Life

The practices of mindfulness and meditation can transform your life. There is literally nothing that you cannot change with these contemplative practices. The reason for this is that everything that we experience is a reflection of our inner world. However, for these transformative experiences to occur, one needs to practice with consistency and joy. What does it mean to practice with consistency and joy? It means to incorporate mediation and mindfulness in your life. Consistency means that you practice daily. By practicing daily, you develop a habit, and that habit becomes part of your lifestyle.

The more you practice, the more that you will get out of it. The more you get out of it, the more joy that you will experience. In turn, joy leads to one giving more of themselves to their practice. It is this giving that changes one's life. In this chapter, you learned how to practice mindfulness and meditation. In the next chapter, you will learn how to balance your chakras.

Chapter 10: Balancing Your Chakras

In Chapter 5, the seven chakras were discussed. Chakras are the energy centers of the body. Our emotional and physical well-being is dependent upon our chakras being balanced. Having balanced chakras is important when it comes to developing your psychic power. The following information provides a brief overview of how to balance your chakras.

The Root Chakra (Muladhara)

When the root chakra is overstimulated, it can lead to issues with the nervous system, including anxiety. The root chakra plays an important role in providing the feeling of security. If you have all your security needs met, the root chakra may be underperforming. This can lead to difficulties in concentrating. For an over stimulated root chakra, develop your connection to your spirit. You can do this by having a daily spiritual practice, such as meditation. If your root chakra is underperforming, spend time in nature. You can also do gardening or spend time walking barefoot outdoors.

The Sacral Chakra (Svadhistana)

When the sacral chakra is overstimulated, one may overindulge in pleasurable activities. This occurs because we have been resistant to experiencing the full range of emotions. Instead, we have only allowed ourselves to experience things that feel good. Conversely, not allowing ourselves to enjoy ourselves can lead to an under-active sacral chakra. This condition can lead to low sex drive, a lack of passion or creativity, and depression. If the sacral chakra is over stimulated, shift your attention to your heart area. This can be accomplished by asking yourself whether the activity you feel like doing would be good for your heart and soul. If the sacral chakra is underperforming, engage in activities that bring you happiness and joy.

The Solar Plexus Chakra (Manipura)

The solar plexus chakra becomes overstimulated when we try to control others. When we try to control others, we are overextending our personal power. Symptoms of an overstimulated solar plexus include being easily angered along with a lack of empathy and compassion for others. The symptoms of an underperforming solar plexus include insecurity, neediness, and being timid. For an over stimulated solar plexus, try opening your heart to others by showing them compassion and empathy. You can also do the exercises in Chapter 9 that involve cultivating super emotions and self-love. If your solar plexus is underperforming, start appreciating yourself by taking notice of your special qualities, abilities, or knowledge. Reflect on what makes you special. You can also say affirmations.

The Heart Chakra (Anahata)

When the heart chakra is overstimulated, one will lose their sense of personal boundaries and become a "people pleaser." They will strive to make others happy while neglecting their own. When the heart chakra is underperforming, one will become cynical of others and feel jaded about love. For the over stimulated heart chakra, one needs to start practicing self-care by establishing personal boundaries. One needs to show the same amount of love toward oneself as one does to others. For the underperforming heart chakra, one needs to extend compassion to others and oneself.

The Throat Chakra (Vishuddi)

An overstimulated throat chakra results from us spending too much time and effort in getting people to listen to us. These efforts are the result of feeling insignificant and invalidated. In the long term, this may lead one to give up trying to express themselves and withhold their truth. When this occurs, one will find difficulty in expressing their emotions or in articulating how they feel. To balance the throat chakra, one needs to learn to speak from a position of integrity. One must start expressing how they feel. Further, one should speak in a manner that respects others and oneself.

The Third Eye Chakra (Ajna)

The third eye chakra is rarely over-stimulated. Normally, when this chakra is not balanced, it is underperforming. This is a common issue in this society as we are not taught to honor our intuition. An underperforming third eye chakra will lead one to feel cut off from their spiritual experiences. In those rare cases where the third eye chakra is overstimulated, one should get in touch with their body and feelings. Get involved in sports, working out, and spending time in nature. Walking barefoot will also help. For an underperforming third eye chakra, one should meditate and journal about their intuitive experiences.

The Crown Chakra (Sahasrara)

While overstimulation of the third eye chakra is rarely a problem, overstimulation of the crown chakra is also never a problem. An underperforming crown chakra is typical of the human species. To raise the functioning of the crown chakra, one needs to balance the remaining six chakras. When this occurs, the crown chakra will be restored to balance.

Affirmations for Balancing Chakras

Affirmations are empowering statements that we make to ourselves with a sense of conviction. By repeating affirmations, one creates a new focal point for the attention. The increased attention leads to the affirmation becoming established in one's belief system.

The following are affirmations for the seven chakras. These affirmations have the power to balance them. When using affirmations, it is important to say them with a sense of emotion and certainty. It can also be helpful to say them while looking into a mirror.

Crown Chakra

- I trust the wisdom of the universe.
- I accept the present moment.
- The power of the universe flows through me.

Third-Eye Chakra

- My wisdom is growing.
- I am learning to trust my intuition.
- I am developing greater clarity in my understanding of life.

Throat Chakra

- I speak my truth.
- I am direct and respectful in my communication.
- I speak from the heart.

Heart Chakra

- I am learning to love and appreciate myself.
- My compassion for others is growing.
- Life's eternal love flows through me.

Solar Plexus Chakra

- I have complete acceptance for my strengths and my weaknesses.
- I am determined to make a difference in life.
- I trust my life and the direction that it is taking me.

Sacral Chakra

- I adapt to whatever life brings my way.
- Life's creativity flows through me.
- I embrace my sexuality.

Root Chakra

- I am feeling balanced and secure in my life.

- I remain stable as my emotions drift by like the clouds.
- I am secure in knowing that life will provide me with what I need.

Conclusion

My hope is that you gained insight from this book regarding your psychic potential. In truth, this book could have been written in a simpler manner. What I mean by this is that this entire book was about pointing to something that you already have— your psychic abilities. Not only do you have psychic powers, but you probably experience them on a daily basis without knowing it. Remember, intuition is a psychic power. This book covered a number of ways in which you can experience your intuition. Use this book as are reference for what you experience and try the exercises to engage with your psychic ability. The development of your psychic abilities is a lifelong process.

www.ingramcontent.com/pod-product-compliance
Lightning Source LLC
Chambersburg PA
CBHW071623030726
47598CB00001B/403